Praise for *Wort/*

A highly entertaining mix of social insight, ethical exploration and practical tips about what constitutes 'wealth' and how to achieve it under your own steam whilst benefiting wider society. A great guide for anyone who wants to improve their life and the world but isn't sure how to take the first step.

Helen Boaden
President of HF Holidays and
former Director of BBC Radio

Dr Bob Gomersall has written an inspirational guide for entrepreneurs to build businesses that allow us to flourish and thrive, rather than just survive, and play a positive role in our planet's future. Drawing on his experiences as a physics teacher and academic turned entrepreneur, Bob shares his successes and failures and uses his scientific background to analyse the risks in starting a business and explains how to mitigate these. As Bob shows, true wealth isn't about cash or status: it's about spending time doing the things you love, being free and having a work life with a sense of purpose at the heart of it.

Dame Linda Pollard
Chair of Leeds Teaching Hospitals NHS Trust

Refreshing. Practical. Inspirational. Special. Bob Gomersall delivers insight, encouragement and understanding from his own experience, and that of others, with intelligent musings from a 'mountain top'. Described, analysed, assessed and presented with insight and encouragement. Best described as wisdom from the real world with advice on how to achieve the satisfaction and reward from a job that is not work but is life, a life in balance with family, friends and community, and yourself. A life of 'worthwhile wealth'.

Brian S. Smith
Former CEO of HF Holidays
Managing Director of Continental Tyres (UK) and
Director of Leyland DAF Trucks

This is a wonderfully stimulating book sharing Bob Gomersall's experience in becoming an entrepreneur, challenging assumptions that profit and wealth should drive work above all, and bringing in social responsibility, ethical, environmental and personal priorities. And it offers many examples of successful entrepreneurship which included these priorities in Yorkshire and the north of England. It's an ideal guide for those thinking about changing direction.

William Wallace
Lord Wallace of Saltaire

A well-timed challenge to wrong thinking that the pursuit of wealth and health might be an zero sum game. Bob, with characteristic rigour and humanity, urges us to understand that we can achieve meaning in our working lives, do some good in this world and also make a few quid. A very readable and grounded philosophy, entertaining too, from a successful entrepreneur with a message about the things that really matter.

Simon Hinchliffe
Headmaster, Bradford Grammar School

DR BOB GOMERSALL

wrth while

WEALTH

An entrepreneur's guide
to success that satisfies

First published in Great Britain by Practical Inspiration Publishing, 2024

ISBN   9781788606301 (hbk)
          9781788606318 (pbk)
          9781788606332 (epub)
          9781788606325 (mobi)

Want to bulk-buy copies of this book for your team and colleagues? We can customize the content and co-brand *Worthwhile Wealth* to suit your business's needs.

Please email info@practicalinspiration.com for more details.

Practical Inspiration Publishing

This book is dedicated to all those wonderful people who have worked with me in physics research, in education and in my various businesses, and who understood implicitly that 'worthwhile wealth' means more than just having money. It is also dedicated to my wife Tricia, my parents and my family, who have all shared this view of life; and especially to my fellow HF Holidays leaders, past and present, who since 1913 have been introducing worthwhile wealth to millions of people through love of the open air and participative social activity.

About the author

Bob Gomersall left a job teaching physics and became an accidental entrepreneur so he could spend more time doing the things he enjoys.

After an initial foray into computer-based tests for teachers, he set up a business building medical equipment. Then he developed computer-based examinations and created one of the world's first educational multimedia CD-ROMs.

Since then, Bob has created multiple companies at the forefront of education and healthcare technology, investing in numerous disruptive technologies. One of his companies won the Queen's Award for Enterprise in international trade. All this while spending as much time as possible walking in the mountains.

Today, when you can't find him on a mountain top, Bob is involved in his role as Chair of Surpass Assessment, a world-leading computer solutions company based in West Yorkshire. Over four decades on, work still feels like a hobby to Bob, because he discovered that 'worthwhile wealth' isn't just about having money.

For a detailed timeline of Bob's career, see the Appendix.

Contents

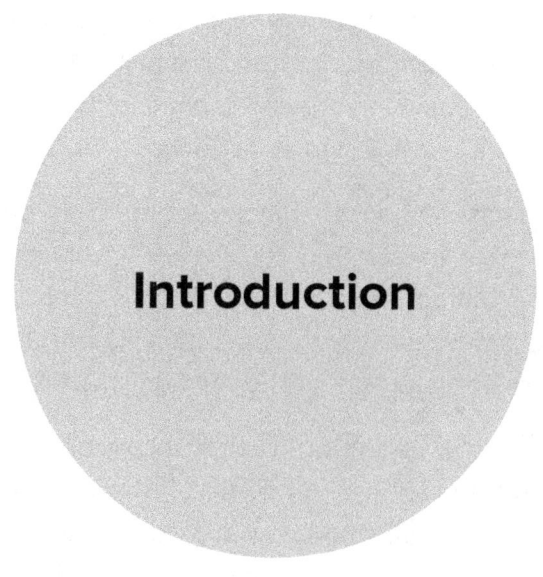

Introduction

Do I enjoy my work?

This is a huge question and one that most people reflect on. Some of us might even ask ourselves this every day before getting out of bed.

The average person spends 35 hours a week working, totting up nearly 90,000 hours over a lifetime. So, naturally, finding a job we love is fundamental to a happy, satisfying existence. But for many of us, the blind, unthinking pursuit of money and status is the driving force behind career choices, rather than consideration of what we would *really* like to do.

If we are lucky enough to have a job we enjoy and work we love, we are indeed fortunate – but that is not the case for many folk.

I am a former physics teacher and academic who became an entrepreneur by accident. Forty years ago, my main interests were physics, teaching, computers, rock climbing and walking in mountains, but none of these different pursuits looked like a promising start to a new business.

These passions, however, led me to set up many successful enterprises that have employed over 450 people and won the Queen's Enterprise Award. My business life has created disruptive innovations in the education and health sector and helped other start-up businesses along the way.

In the beginning, I set out to change the way I worked but never set out to earn a lot of money. Instead, I aligned my own values with growing a business of genuine personal interest and focused my spare time on doing things I love.

For the past 50 years, I have led hiking holidays with HF Holidays, where I've met people from all walks of life, including many highly successful businesspeople. It's amazing what folk will confide in you when sitting at the top of a hill or mountain.

Admiring the view, sharing the odd snack, I heard incredible stories of what makes people tick and what effect their work has on their lives. Some told me what makes their jobs feel purposeful and valuable, while others talked about why they made life-changing career decisions. Some walkers moaned and groaned about spending a lifetime in a job they hate, wondering what it's all for. Others retired with huge financial wealth but little peace of mind.

A surprising number confided that despite achieving huge 'success' on paper, they feel deeply dissatisfied. The stories I heard gave me huge insight into what makes work fulfilling and what creates what I call 'worthwhile wealth'.

What makes people flourish in life? What does flourishing even mean? Is it possible to start up a business that brings genuine pleasure? Does running a business with a value or purpose behind it make a difference? Time and again, the same ideas crop up.

Worthwhile wealth, I discovered, isn't about cash or status. It's about time and, vitally, spending that time doing things you love. It's about having the freedom to do what you want when you want. And having a work life with a sense of purpose at the heart of it.

Today, more and more leaders and big thinkers share this view. Increasingly, the idea is that achieving economic growth at any cost no longer works for the well-being of citizens, not least because constant growth is draining our planet of resources and is providing very few people with the quality of life they long for.

Times are hard. The cost of living crisis, inflation and Brexit have rocked standards of living in the UK. Climate change is the biggest challenge humankind will ever face. So, is this really the time to be considering anything but survival?

Yes. In fact, it's even more vital. For what we do on a micro level affects the global level. We are all part of the bigger picture, and how we earn money plays a role in our planet's future.

Building a business – small or large – that allows us to flourish and thrive, rather than just survive, needn't be a pipe dream. The internet, working from home and access to huge support networks have made starting a new business more accessible than ever before.

You might be a person who has never run a business but has always wanted to – a graduate with a big idea who doesn't know where to begin, someone in mid-life who dares 'to dream' but not 'to do' or someone who understands there is more to life than the 'tramlines' many of us blindly follow because we can't quite shake off the shackles. I know how hard this is, because it took me years to shake off the shackles myself.

In this book, I include the stories of entrepreneurs from every walk of life, from business leaders to graduates, tech wizards, a clothes designer, a young single mother and a multimillionaire. All of them were willing to share how they succeeded in finding worthwhile wealth by starting a business with purpose that worked for them.

Step by step, I share my successes and failures. Using my scientific background, I have analysed and unpicked many of the risk factors of starting a business and how to mitigate those risks. I consider the challenges every new entrepreneur will face and examine the importance of innovation, long-term strategy and working ethically. I also discuss how sustainable businesses will help sustain our planet's resources.

If just one person reads this book and is inspired to take the first steps to find true wealth and build a flourishing business, it's been worth writing.

Hopefully, theories and ideas from these pages will set you on the right path, towards whatever mountains you wish to conquer.

What creates 'worthwhile wealth'?

In this chapter, I examine:

- The value of money
- What makes human beings flourish
- The concept behind 'worthwhile wealth'

The joy some people get from driving a flashy car is not even a hundredth of that some people get from walking for pleasure.

—Mokokoma Mokhonoana

If I were to ask what it means to be wealthy, how would most people reply?

They might say that it's to afford holidays to far-flung places, to own a large fancy house, to drive a flash car, to buy a yacht to sail around the world...

To me, this is what it means to *spend* lots of money. Why do people keep striving long after they have enough money to live well? My conclusion is that money motivates not in the clichéd way of fancy cars, yachts, planes, etc., but as a measure of performance.

This applies even to the *spending* of money. Beyond a certain level of wealth, people spend money to show how well they have done rather than to have something of intrinsic value. Money doesn't buy you happiness. How often have you heard that phrase? Well, money buys you happiness *to a point*…

A well-known study by Daniel Kahneman and Angus Deaton from Princeton University, published in 2010, revealed that day-to-day happiness rose until a salary of around $75,000 (£61,000) per annum was reached, and then it plateaued.[1] However, another study headed by Matthew Killingsworth from the University of Pennsylvania discovered that happiness rose steadily beyond a salary of $75,000, without a plateau.[2] So, three academics – Kahneman, Killingsworth and another, Barbara Mellers – got together to further explore the data on this.[3]

---

[1] See Michele W. Berger, Does money buy happiness? Here's what the research says, *Knowledge at Wharton* (28 March 2023), https://knowledge.wharton.upenn.edu/article/does-money-buy-happiness-heres-what-the-research-says (accessed 19 March 2024).

[2] Matthew A. Killingsworth, Experienced well-being rises with income, even above $75,000 per year, *PNAS*, 118(4): e2016976118 (2021), www.pnas.org/doi/abs/10.1073/pnas.2016976118 (accessed 19 March 2024).

[3] Matthew A. Killingsworth, Daniel Kahneman and Barbara Mellers, Income and emotional well-being: a conflict resolved, *PNAS*, 120(10): e2208661120 (2023), https://pubmed.ncbi.nlm.nih.gov/36857342/ (accessed 19 March 2024).

They also found that higher incomes show an increase in happiness, but in their analysis, this plateaus abruptly when salary reaches $100,000 (£82,000); they also found that if you were unhappy anyway, money would not solve your problems.

These studies reveal that wealth doesn't alter certain personal habits either. If you were a spendthrift before you made a million, you will still be a big spender, and if you were generous, being rich won't change that.

Essentially, money doesn't miraculously change a person's behaviour for the better.

In my experience of watching peers become very wealthy, something curious happens to many of them. Once they've had a few nice holidays and bought the big house and fancy car, they mostly end up asking '*What's next?*'

Even for the super-rich – say, those earning over $500,000 – wealth doesn't automatically bring happiness. I remember reading how the billionaire Jeff Bezos, one of the richest men on the planet, commissioned the world's tallest sailing yacht for an eye-watering sum of $500 million.[4] It cost over $100,000 a day to run. But this wasn't enough, so Bezos bought an accompanying boat with a helicopter pad and

---

[4] Lee Brown, Jeff Bezos buys $500M superyacht amid luxury industry boom, *New York Post* (10 May 2021), https://nypost.com/2021/05/10/jeff-bezos-superyacht-costs-500m-amid-luxury-industry-boom (accessed 19 March 2024).

a submarine, and employed a crew of 45 people to be on standby next to it.[5]

This sort of extravagance is astonishing to most of us, but the example isn't about criticizing what rich people spend their brass on. Rather, the story reveals how the pursuit of spending money on 'stuff' can be endless.

(Interestingly, the sail on Bezos's yacht was so tall that when he needed to move it from Holland, his people asked permission to temporarily dismantle the Koningshaven Bridge, which had survived Second World War bombings. This triggered a protest and 5,000 Dutch people signed up to throw eggs at the yacht. But I digress...)

The point here is that the pursuit of money is limitless and rarely brings the sense of satisfaction we are led, brainwashed in fact, to believe it will.

Indeed, money can even make life feel *less* satisfying. After all, society teaches us that if we become rich, all our cares in the world will fade away, but time (and academic studies!) reveals this simply isn't true. Perhaps his superyacht made Bezos super satisfied. Or perhaps not... I haven't asked him, but I'd put money on it being unlikely.

How often have we read stories about lottery winners who end up unhappy and broke? How many true tales are there

---

[5] 9 surprising facts about Jeff Bezos' new mega yacht Koru, *Style* (12 March 2023), www.scmp.com/magazines/style/celebrity/ article/3213036/9-surprising-facts-about-jeff-bezos-new-mega-yacht-koru-it-cost-us500-million-size-2-airbus-a380s (accessed 25 March 2024).

of rich and famous people struggling with loneliness and mental health problems despite having wealth beyond their wildest dreams? Or of young, overworked bankers under so much pressure that they tragically decide to end it all? All around us there is proof that money, especially huge sums, doesn't buy us satisfaction in life.

Incredible as it sounds, from my observations, many wealthy people simply don't even know what to spend their hard-earned money on. I once asked a fellow walker how his retirement was going and he confessed to remortgaging his house to buy back into his business.

Like freedom, wealth too is relative. For example, if you earn a million a year but have expensive tastes and find yourself spending over a million each year, then you're in debt and will need more money.

We can conclude that 'worthwhile wealth' is not found by making more and more money.

Case study: tales from a mountain top

T.A. Leonard is a great example of someone who recognized worthwhile wealth. Between 1893 and 1926, he built up two incredibly successful holiday businesses that, by the end of that period, provided over 60,000 holidays a year and owned 60 valuable country house properties in beautiful locations.

The remarkable thing is that he took nothing more than a modest income out of these businesses, which were configured as cooperatives. Even more remarkable – and fundamental to their success – was the fact that the businesses focused on two key elements of what I think worthwhile wealth brings: social interactions between people and love of the outdoors. Indeed, he was often associated with the phrase 'the greatest thing which any mortal hath is that which every mortal shares'.

Perhaps this sounds a little old-fashioned today, but that is our loss. Leonard was particularly keen on fostering international goodwill through people of different nations meeting on holiday, and he was instrumental in the formation of the Youth Hostels Association in 1930 and the Ramblers Association in 1935.

When he retired, he was asked what gift he would like. He asked for a large country house in Patterdale in the Lake District, which he then gifted to the Youth Hostels Association.

His legacy lives on in HF Holidays, a successful cooperative providing sociable walking holidays, enjoyed by people of many nations.

Money buys us food, shelter, experiences and what many believe is security. These things are all important for some people's peace of mind and I do not make light of the necessity of having enough money to live off. We all need enough to live comfortably, and in the current cost of living crisis (or 'low wage' crisis as it should be called), it costs more than ever to cover the basics.

The concepts in this book challenge some of the ideas we have been led to believe in. I question what makes life worth living and what kind of work brings us most pleasure and satisfaction, and why growth (of all kinds) at any cost is no longer the answer.

Time is money

Money is a store of value. It is also something human beings have agreed to exchange as a tool to make trade more efficient. And its value only matters when we choose to spend it. Nobody works all hours to store their money in a bank and never touch it.

Most people who earn huge wealth, like the financiers, will be at someone else's bidding for a lot of their time. They must be at a certain place and work around others' schedules, complying with heavy demands and expectations. Time and freedom for those in high-powered jobs is very limited. That's a big price to pay.

Henry David Thoreau said, 'Wealth is the ability to fully experience life.' What do you want to do to fully experience life? Pursue a business dream? Invent something? Travel? Spend more time with family? Enjoy a passion every day? Master a skill set? Have more time to read all the novels you love? Go for a walk in the mountains?

For years, I have helped run HF Holidays. The business, set up in 1913, is a not-for-profit company that promotes walking and socializing. It is phenomenally successful. We have over 700 walking leaders and are never short of people to volunteer. But why is that? It's because it's immense fun. It feels good for the soul to be outdoors in the natural world, and, my goodness, of all the places to hang out, a mountain top is hard to beat. We all can flourish up there.

'Flourish' is one of my favourite words. There are plenty of ways to find worthwhile wealth that help us to flourish in this life. Nature flourishes and so can we, but often living life on autopilot, doggedly pursuing money and status, holds us back.

What makes human beings flourish?

Everyone's idea of flourishing will be personal to them, but over the years when I've talked to people about this, similar themes have cropped up. Once we have all our immediate needs met – food, shelter, purpose, social needs – then what is necessary to make life feel enriched? The most common things include:

- Having a good social life
- Showing kindness to yourself and others
- Keeping fit and healthy
- Having peace of mind
- Having a strong sense of belonging
- Enjoying deeper relationships with those around us
- Having the time and head space to enjoy the small pleasures in life

- Having freedom to make decisions you want to make when you want to make them
- Working in an interesting job that feels purposeful

My personal list includes: spending time with my family and friends; working with people I like; living in an area of the country I love (Yorkshire); running a company that improves the lives of others; and having time to pursue my favourite hobbies, which of course include walking in mountains.

The concept of worthwhile wealth

Accomplishments in life that go unnoticed to other people are often the ones that provide us with the most pleasure.

Examples include enjoying deep, long-lasting friendships, having successful relationships with family members, pursuing a passion, making a difference to a child or someone vulnerable, and feeling connected and valued by people in your community. It's authentic connections and freedoms that makes us feel good.

To build on this, creating work that has a meaningful impact on our everyday life is arguably one of the best ways to find worthwhile wealth. Experiencing the flow of creativity in your job, being able to create a product or service you feel genuine pride in and reaching goals that give a sense of meaning to your working life are accomplishments we don't often examine the value of.

Worthwhile wealth comes from having options. It means having time, which in turn means having energy. Energy to do things you love doing. No doubt monetary wealth creates options, but it could require many lost years to be in this position. Far better to think about devoting your life to things that you consider worthwhile. That is indeed worthwhile wealth. This is more sustainable because the motivation is ever-present and it is almost always better for us, for both our physical and our mental well-being. It's the opposite of burnout, disillusionment and isolation, which is what modern ways of working and living lead to for many.

Setting up my own business was never motivated by money. Rather, I wanted to live near great countryside, in nice surroundings, and to be able to do things that were creative and that interested me. In brief, I wanted to do the things that I wanted to do.

If I define work as that which I do **not** wish to do, then I did not want to work. I did not want to be told what work to do or be told where to live. That's why I left the world of academia and, eventually, teaching.

Chances are that finding work with meaning doesn't involve a job in finance or indeed many of the jobs in the private and public sectors. So, what does it involve? This is where I make my argument that following your entrepreneurial spirit, something we all possess, is where worthwhile wealth can be found. It's wealth in the widest sense, which creates value for us and our communities.

*

Deciding what worthwhile wealth means to you personally will bring clarity to what sort of thriving business idea to pursue.

Here is how I define the main components to experiencing worthwhile wealth:

- Finding employment that is sustaining for all immediate needs
- Doing work that is useful to society
- Having time to pursue interests or passions
- Living where you want to live
- Feeling in control of your destiny
- Living as sustainably as possible

What would be on your worthwhile wealth list? The 'Ideas into action' section at the end of the book has a series of questions which might help you focus your answers.

Case study: tales from a mountain top

Jane Ascroft was good at maths at school, so her father suggested she find a 'proper job' and become an accountant, then build a small team of employees. But despite spending decades in the profession and running a successful accountancy business, Jane longed to try other ventures. When Jane's personal circumstances changed, she reinvented her working life and created time to do what she really wanted to do...

Several events occurred at once that made me decide to change everything. First, I went on a holiday to the mountains in Morocco with friends who were qualified mountain leaders. I watched them and realized that I had the skills and experience to do what they were doing.

I'd always loved the mountains, walking and climbing from an early age, but how could I go from being an accountant to a mountain leader?

Then, in quick succession, big life events happened. I got divorced, my father died and my mother came to live near me, as she needed extra support. Suddenly I was a single mum with caring responsibilities and struggling to work full time. To top things off, I caught Covid-19 quite badly, and the recovery took a long time, making it harder than ever to tolerate sitting in front of a computer screen.

I was forced to reduce my workload and, overnight, I went from working 45 hours a week to 15 hours a week. I was very worried that my business would fold, but my employees and clients were loyal and supportive and over the next two years my business stabilized. Every cloud has a silver lining – now I had the time to follow my dreams. I qualified as a mountain leader and joined the local mountain rescue team.

Today, I still work 15 hours a week in accountancy and spend the rest of my time juggling a variety of jobs – caring for my mum and daughter, volunteering for mountain rescue and putting my mountain leader skills to good use. When I'm in the mountains, leading or with the mountain rescue team, I feel that this is what I was supposed to do with my life.

My accountancy background has come in useful, in particular my managerial skills, communication skills and an ability to stay calm under pressure and to think in a strategic way.

When I met Bob on a walking holiday, he asked if I ever planned to expand my business and my answer was 'Absolutely not!' Keeping my team small and working part time works for me, rather than me working for it.

I choose to see 'risks' as 'opportunities' and have always tried to make the most of what comes along.

Life is short. Nobody is going to hand you what you want and how you want it on a plate. Opportunities to make life more meaningful need to be seized while you can.

Further reading

Daniel Kahneman, *Thinking, Fast and Slow* (2011).

John Williams, *Screw Work, Let's Play* (2010).

Ong Boon Hwee and Mark Goyder, *Entrusted: Stewardship for Responsible Wealth Creation* (2020).

2

The unlikely entrepreneur

In this chapter, I examine:

- What motivates ordinary people to start a business
- What characteristics are necessary to be a successful entrepreneur
- How to identify your personal motivation drivers

I believe we are all unlikely entrepreneurs. Many people do not realize that the skill set needed to set up a business is part of their natural disposition. Observe any child and their ability to pester their parents to get what they want out of life and it's clear. For example, if an ice cream van is close by, any kid can immediately come up with 20 reasons why they deserve a Flake 99 ice cream, and they will keep persuading their parents until they get that sale.

When I showed my class my first invention, an audiometer, one of the boys quipped, 'Can you paint it a pastel shade and sell it for twice the price, Sir?' – once again proving kids make natural entrepreneurs.

What our motivation is for starting a small business lies at the heart of whether it will be a success or not.

Finding worthwhile wealth can be a big motivating factor and is arguably the best one there is. But what else motivates people? Daniel Pink, in his book *Drive*, states: 'We have three innate psychological needs—competence, autonomy, and relatedness. When those needs are satisfied, we're motivated, productive, and happy.'

He argues that if a person feels autonomous, it leads to engagement with their task.

If they feel competent in what they're doing and reap the rewards, they will keep wanting to do it. If they feel connected and part of a network and community of people, they're more likely to enjoy what they're doing.

Digging deep and understanding your own psychological reasoning for taking the plunge with a new business is what will help sustain you when the inevitable challenges arise.

Mountains of motivation

'Why do you want to climb Everest?' asked a newspaper reporter.

'Because it's there.'

Originally this pithy response was thought to be the words of Edmund Hillary before he and Tenzing Norgay conquered Mount Everest in 1953. But it was the lesser-known climber George Mallory who uttered these famous words three decades earlier, in 1924, when he was preparing to climb the world's highest peak.[6]

---

[6] 'Because it's there', *Forbes* (29 October 2001), www.forbes.com/global/2001/1029/060.html?sh=71d53e522080 (accessed 19 March 2024).

The poor lad and his climbing partner perished on the Northeast Ridge and their bodies were not discovered until 75 years later. Nobody even knows whether they made it to the top or not. Despite the tragedy of the story, 'because it's there' remains a legendary reply to an open-ended question and reveals a lot about a person's motivation.

Sometimes seeking adventure or following the path less travelled is enough of a reason to try something.

Similarly, when asked the reasons for starting a business, an entrepreneur might reply:

'Because I want to do a job that involves my hobby.'

'Because I want a job with a purpose.'

'Because I want to work around my kids.'

'Because I want to make a difference.'

'Because I want to find meaning in my work life.'

'Because I see a gap in the market and think I can do better.'

The reasons for climbing a mountain and starting a business are endless, and all are valid to the individual.

Both climbers and entrepreneurs need similar motivating drivers to make a success of their endeavour. These include:

- **Grit.** To finish a climb or take the plunge with a new venture, resilience and persistence is essential.
- **Being proactive and action-orientated.** To keep going to reach a peak, you must take action; you also need enthusiasm, self-belief, passion and energy. A long-term strategy plays a part in this. You must

prepare before going climbing in the same way you must prepare to start a business. This is to pace energy and drive so you don't run out of steam halfway. Momentum needs to keep you going!

- **Relying on team effort.** Walking alone in the mountains is generally considered inadvisable. In business, you must find mentors, team workers and a supportive network too. Being able to communicate your needs and be open-minded to adapt to changing conditions is as vital on a mountain as it is in building a business.

- **Celebrating small wins.** Stopping to admire the view makes any long walk worthwhile, as does celebrating the small successes in a start-up. If we don't admire the view or celebrate our accomplishments on the way, the journey will be less enjoyable and rewarding.

- **Flexibility.** On any walk you must be open to the idea of changing circumstances, changing weather patterns and any other risks that may come up. An entrepreneur must also keep innovation at the forefront of their mind, because business is an environment of constant change.

- **Creative and innovative thinking.** To adapt to the environment, walkers must be creative about the paths they take. Similarly, an entrepreneur must consider a mitigating risk plan, and think creatively to confront inevitable challenges.

Lure of the money men

In *Other People's Money*, John Kay poses some interesting questions about making money a priority. He talks about how people who work in finance reap little satisfaction from their jobs, aside from achieving their goal of making money so they can retire early. 'What might these individuals have done,' he asks, 'if they had not been offered the prospect of huge rewards?'

This is what I have observed. I have three sons and a daughter. Three went to the University of Cambridge and one, like me, saw Durham as a better bet. All have become engineers, and two have started their own business. Proud dad I am!

However, almost all their graduate friends went into finance – or were lured into finance, should I say, by the relentless marketing of companies on the milk round looking to poach the brightest and best graduates.

John Kay agrees with this.

> For three decades a high proportion of the ablest graduates in the country have been attracted by startlingly large salaries into activities of little value to business or society. Activities that did little to develop their skills, knowledge or intellectual capacity except in the narrowest of areas. How might their lives and Britain's economy and society have differed if this financialization had not occurred?

So, what does this mean for our society? What does it mean for the lives of talented young people who are not conscious of what worthwhile wealth could provide?

I wonder how much talent is wasted in the pursuit of money alone when we could be pursuing valuable contributions to society, climate change, our communities. It's little wonder either that rates of anxiety, depression and stress are at epidemic levels when the question 'what do I really want to do?' isn't even contemplated.

And what becomes of the money goal? Do people have to wait for retirement to catch up on the things they would or could have loved to do?

This reminds me of a fable…

*

In a small coastal village, there is a fisherman peacefully casting his net from a small boat. One evening, after fishing all afternoon, he rows back to shore with his boat full of fish.

An intrigued businessman has been watching the fisherman from the shore and approaches him. 'How long does it usually take you to catch this many fish?'

'Maybe a couple of hours,' the fisherman replies.

The businessman's eyes light up. He sees potential in this as an investment opportunity.

'I can give you money for a bigger boat so you can set up your own company, and then we can do a deal to supply all the eateries in the area with your fish.'

Puzzled, the fisherman looks at him. 'And then what?'

The businessman thinks and then excitedly suggests more. 'How about we try and export the fish further afield, to other cities and towns nearby!'

The fisherman stares at him. 'And then…?' he asks.

The businessman is in his stride. 'And then we get investors interested in buying the company for a huge sum and split the deal.'

The fisherman stares again. 'What happens next?'

The businessman laughs. 'You'll be so well off you can do whatever you want. Move to a house by the sea, fish all day long if you like!'

It was the fisherman's turn to laugh. 'That's what I do already.'

(Source unknown)

What are your motivation drivers?

> People should pursue what they're passionate about. That will make them happier than pretty much anything else.
>
> —Elon Musk

Identifying what your personal motivation drivers are will help you decide on the best business to bring you worthwhile wealth.

A few years ago, I joined a supportive business network called The Alternative Board where groups of CEOs get together to help one another with problems and share stories. One of the founding members in the UK, Jo Clarkson, describes how she chooses what businesses to work with by considering business and personal drivers: 'The front wheel of your bike should be your personal vision and set out your direction with what you want out of life. The back wheel should be your business, which helps power you to get what you want.'

Like Jo, I divide motivation drivers (which I list below as a series of 'M's) into business and personal categories.

Business motivation drivers include:

- **Making Money.** Without a doubt we need money to survive, so this must be included, but no successful entrepreneur I know began with this as a sole motivation. Be wary if money is your only objective, as this can feel motivating to begin with but is unlikely to sustain you unless you also find a sense of purpose and value within the business.
- **Following Market demand.** If you have been working inside an industry for a while, you might have noticed a demand that has not been met within the market. This is a common driver for people in mid-life who are established in a career. The advantage of pursuing a market-led business is knowing that a market already exists for this product.
- **Making a Modification.** You might have spotted a market for a service or product that could be tweaked to improve the customer experience, or you might know how to improve on the quality of a product. Could the product be developed more sustainably or could products already in use be recycled, for example?
- **Making a change for the better.** Social enterprise is a huge motivator for many start-ups. A product or service that helps people or makes life easier drives change from grassroots level.
- **Following My idea or My invention.** You might have a great idea – maybe one that no one else has

thought of or one that is a major improvement on what already exists – and simply want to see it used by people.

Personal motivation drivers include:

- **Making time.** Time is the currency we use to do what we like, to devote to family, hobbies, interests or other ambitions. Will your start-up free up time by allowing you to choose the hours to suit your lifestyle outside of work?
- **Mastering something.** This could involve a market you're already working in – you can see how an idea or concept could be taken further and you have the skills to master it. Working for oneself can mean reaping more satisfying rewards than trying to work for a corporate where inventions and visions are not necessarily welcomed. Have you reached a certain career stage where you cannot go any further and a start-up could reinvigorate your ambition? Do you want to master a skill set but your current role holds you back?
- **Moving to a different field or area.** You might want to move to a different field of work, or relocate to another area of the country or the world, and starting a company is one way of doing this.
- **Managing your own time.** You might want to manage your own company, feel like a master of your own destiny or manage other elements of your life better.
- **Maintaining what you have while building something new.** You might want to maintain

a full-time job and start a side hustle to try and build a dream business slowly, or you might have a passion project that might not make enough money to pay the bills but is its own reward.

Case study: tales from a mountain top

Dave Stewart had been working as a science teacher when he had a nervous breakdown. Unsure what to do next, he went to a life coach for advice. It turned out to be a very short appointment…

The life coach asked me, 'What do you enjoy doing the most?', and I replied, 'Singing.'

I had always sung in choirs for as long as I remember. It brought me so much joy.

'What is your greatest skill set?' she then asked.

'Teaching,' I replied.

Then she stared at me and smiled until, very quickly, the penny dropped.

Could I teach singing? This seemed a perfect solution. At first the idea almost seemed too obvious, and overwhelming. After all, where would I start?

Around the same time, I came across an inspirational quote from Goethe, in a passage by William Hutchison Murray:

Until one is committed, there is hesitancy, the chance to draw back, always ineffectiveness. Concerning all acts of initiative (and creation), there is one elementary truth the ignorance of which kills countless ideas and splendid plans: that the moment one definitely commits oneself, then Providence moves too. All sorts of things occur to help one that would never have otherwise occurred. A whole stream of events issues from the decision, raising in one's favour all manner of unforeseen incidents, meetings and material assistance, which no man could have dreamt would have come his way. I have learned a deep respect for one of Goethe's couplets:

Whatever you can do, or dream you can, begin it. Boldness has genius, power and magic in it![7]

The quote really moved me, and I realized from then on I had to follow my passion and hope the doors would open to me. I also knew I never wanted to work for someone else again.

My wife had done a similar thing years earlier when she gave up her job as a lecturer and set up her own massage therapy business. I supported her back then and she agreed to support me with my new endeavour. Suddenly, I realized the nervous breakdown was the best thing that could have happened.

---

[7] William Hutchison Murray, *The Scottish Himalayan Expedition* (1951).

Before then, I never questioned what I wanted to do or who I wanted to be. I came from a middle-class family and was expected to get a job, a mortgage, have a family and then one day retire. The first job I landed was in structural engineering, but I gave that up to become a teacher. Now I realized neither job made me happy.

What happens when your computer goes wrong? You turn it off and on again and wait for it to restart. This deletes any previous conflict and restarts with a clean slate. So that's what I did after talking to that life coach, and when I turned on again, I knew I had to pursue something I love.

Within months, I set up Sing Out, and Liz, my wife, helped me. The idea was to encourage the active participation in singing rather than passive consumption.

We set up four choirs, singing music from folk traditions around the world, and decided to run it on a subscription basis.

It was a slow start but soon built up traction by word of mouth. Teaching others the joy of singing feels like the place I am meant to be. Today we run events including singing holidays in places as far away as Greece and Turkey.

My job now isn't work to me; it is my life. Singing is part of being human as we learned to sing before language even existed. Singing is just who I am, what I love, and seeing the immense pleasure it brings to other people makes it all worthwhile.

Further reading

John Kay, *Other People's Money: Masters of the Universe or Servants of the People?* (2015).

Daniel Pink, *Drive: The Surprising Truth about What Motivates Us* (2010).

3

Challenging the national discourse

In this chapter, I examine:

- How cultural influences affect our self-belief
- Why it's important to challenge the status quo
- Why popular economic models don't work

The national discourse includes theories, cultural norms and ideas we are all familiar with but are not encouraged to question, especially when pursuing a new start-up idea and worthwhile wealth.

If we are to build businesses that flourish, we must challenge the status quo, because much of it doesn't work for society at large or indeed entrepreneurs. Politicians exhort us business founders to work hard to create more money, presumably so they can get more taxes out of us. Yet most of the entrepreneurs I know say they are not motivated by money.

It therefore suits a wealthy few for a lot of the national discourse not to be challenged at all. In addition, the exercise of power at a national level involves little more than allocating money, and so generation of growth is necessary to feed this.

Yet messages communicated from the education system, media, government, institutions and society in general have a powerful and lasting impact on how business is run. By identifying what messages are unhelpful, we can discern what discourse serves us better and forge our own paths more confidently.

So, what are the big national discourse points to challenge?

The national discourse on... education

> Education is what remains after one has forgotten what one has learned in school.
>
> —Einstein

It's often said that your schooldays are the best days of your life. Really? Not for everyone. Our experience at school has a profound subconscious effect on the way we view ourselves and our strengths and weaknesses, and even whether we consider ourselves capable of running a business.

Who believes they are 'no good' at certain subjects like maths (and therefore would struggle to start a business)? Who was always told off for daydreaming in class? Who didn't pass their A levels so deep down considers themselves to be a little stupid? We often build assumptions about our strengths and weaknesses from our classroom days that carry through to adulthood.

The education process tends to value the ability to focus, whether the student is interested or not. This is great for creating professionals – accountants, lawyers and so on –

but is not helpful for many other areas and certainly not for being an entrepreneur.

At school, one teacher stands in front of the desks imparting their wisdom, or at least regurgitating information from textbooks. I call it factory learning, because it's a one-size-fits-all approach that doesn't cater for individual needs. The reality is that teaching methods have hardly changed since mass education began.

Kids are told at school that to be a success in life, they must pass standardized examinations. I see this as imposing 'tramlines' which we are conditioned to follow into adulthood and our careers.

At the start of the tramline, kids are ranked, and this determines their access to the next level. This ranking continues up through each stage in their education. Competition is encouraged, and we all grow up to understand who a winner and loser is, who passes and who fails. This ideology is then taken forward into our adult lives, neatly carrying us on to the employment tramline journey, where the winners become wealthy and have status.

But winning or losing is never binary, especially in business.

Cath Bishop, author of *The Long Win*, is a three-time Olympic rower who won medals at two World Championships and an Olympic silver medal. She believes, however, that our cultural obsession with so-called 'winning' in education, sports and work doesn't bring the fulfilment we're led to believe it will. Instead, finding purpose, authentic relationships and focus on personal growth is immensely more rewarding.

She says: 'Many countries still have rigid systems of testing and narrowly chartered education paths, which bear no resemblance to lifetime experiences, or the attributes needed in the modern workplace.' In short, the ingrained fixation on winning, especially when it comes to the way we teach our kids, actually holds us back.

I worked as a teacher for 20 years and loved the job, but I couldn't agree more with Cath's statement. Creativity, lateral thinking and a wandering mind are all brilliant traits in a budding entrepreneur, but in children they can be viewed as bad behaviour.

*

Einstein said: 'Most people say that is it is the intellect which makes a great scientist. They are wrong: it is character.' I believe this applies to entrepreneurs too.

The kids who rebelled in class made me laugh and I admired their creative thinking. Once, a fellow teacher rolled his eyes when he spotted one of my wayward students had achieved good test results against the odds.

'I can see Robert has done it again,' he frowned with disapproval.

I laughed and replied, 'I can see Robert succeeding in life far better than any of us will.' And that was because he didn't adhere to the tramlines.

There are so many examples of successful entrepreneurs who did not do well, in the conventional sense, at school. Richard Branson was dyslexic, dropped out and set up a student paper, eventually entering the music business and then going on to become a global business icon. He lives on a tropical island now and is often at the forefront of social enterprises, no doubt enjoying worthwhile wealth.

Pimlico Plumbers boss, Charlie Mullins, left school at 15 without qualifications and went from having a 'man in a van' set-up to having a business worth over £70 million. He has commented: 'it's over-promoted, the university side of it. There's life without a degree.'[8]

Deborah Meaden, star of BBC TV show *Dragons' Den*, ditched the idea of A levels and instead went to business college and, aged 19, set up her own start-up. She went on to build a ceramics business, which she sold to Harvey Nichols, then a holiday business, which she sold to focus on helping other entrepreneurs – something that no doubt brings her enormous satisfaction.

Sharon Peacock, Professor of Public Health and Microbiology at the University of Cambridge, failed her 11 Plus exam and wasn't allowed to take the science exams she needed for medical school. Only after training as a dental nurse did she manage to go to night school to pass the exams. Even then, she was refused entry to the course she needed. In the end, Sharon phoned the University of Southampton to speak directly to an admissions tutor to ask them why. Luckily, the

---

[8] Naomi Ackerman, Five entrepreneurs and CEOs who didn't do A-levels but made it to the top, *The Standard* (10 August 2021), www.standard.co.uk/business/ceos-and-entrepreneurs-no-a-levels-but-made-it-to-the-top-b950047.html (accessed 19 March 2024).

tutor recognized her ambitious spark and took a chance by giving her a place on the course.

In her recent interview on BBC Radio 4's *Desert Island Discs*, Sharon talked about having a guiding principle of wanting to give 'public service'.[9] Admirably, her sense of social purpose is her main motivational driver for pursuing her passion.

There are countless other entrepreneurs operating on a smaller scale who completely turned their backs on a traditional education or career, hopping off the tramlines to find something more fulfilling.

I am not saying education is a bad thing – far from it. Indeed, the more you know, especially in science and engineering, the more opportunities you will have to create innovative enterprises. It does sometimes seem, however, that the further you have gone down the educational tramlines the harder it is to jump off and transfer that knowledge to create a business of value.

Think about these questions: What beliefs did you leave school with? Could you challenge those beliefs today? Will any of those beliefs hold you back when it comes to setting up a business?

Bob's musings from a mountain top

For years, always at the bottom of the class when it came to speed arithmetic tests, I considered myself hopeless at maths.

---

[9] BBC Radio 4, Professor Sharon Peacock, scientist [audio], *Desert Island Discs*, www.bbc.co.uk/programmes/m001m4nx (accessed 10 March 2024).

It wasn't until I did a PhD in theoretical physics that I realized I am actually pretty good at sums, but I am not a fast thinker. I am a slow thinker by nature. That's a general trait with lots of physicists. We must be, because we need to slowly work things out step by step so that we can be confident at each stage of learning. It's when students miss out a step in physics that they struggle to understand the concepts.

Niels Bohr, who first explained the structure of the atom, was a great fan of cowboy films, but was also notorious for his inability to follow the plot, pestering those with him for explanations. In essence, different people have unique and different skill sets. You could be a quiet, slow-thinking introvert or a loud, artistic, scatty visionary but still create an incredible business. Basic business skills can be learned by anyone.

The national discourse on... economic models

> The financial markets generally are unpredictable. So that one has to have different scenarios... The idea that you can actually predict what's going to happen contradicts my way of looking at the market.
>
> —George Soros[10]

Conventional economics has got so much wrong. Most economic models originate from over 100 years ago, and since the 1970s the finance sector has taken more risk, but

---

[10] PBS, Interview with George Soros, *Frontline*, www.pbs.org/wgbh/pages/frontline/shows/crash/interviews/soros.html (accessed 19 March 2024).

with other people's money. Growth for the sake of it is still viewed as the main measure of success.

Understanding why popular economic models don't work helps us understand why many jobs don't create value, purpose or worthwhile wealth.

Take the finance sector, for example. We are told that it is needed to pay taxes for public services – but many of these institutions simply move money around. In *Other People's Money*, John Kay says:

> The value of the assets underlying derivative contracts is three times the value of all the physical assets in the world. What is it all for? What is the purpose of this activity? And why is it so profitable? Common sense suggests that if a closed circle of people continuously exchange bits of paper with each other, the total value of these bits of paper will not change much, if at all. If some members of that closed circle make extraordinary profits, these profits can only be made at the expense of other members of the same circle. Common sense suggests that this activity leaves the value of the traded assets little changed, and cannot, taken as a whole, make money.

The concept of the 'rational economic man', or *Homo economicus*, is also a rather ludicrous cornerstone of economics. The idea of this model is that the average person will always make rational decisions in their self-interest when all possible economic factors are considered. This theory underpins many decisions on incentives in business.

But scientific studies reveal most people base cognitive decisions on emotions and bias, including what is normalized in their social circles, rather than on self-interest only.

For example, some investors may panic and take all their money out when they see markets plunge, even if they stand to lose money in the long run. Or when markets rise, fear of missing out leads others to buy shares despite it being more expensive. How many people also make compulsive purchases either to cheer themselves up or to celebrate a success, even if it's unaffordable? We are emotionally driven human beings, not economic model robots.

In conventional economics, businesses are treated as 'black boxes'. Cash goes in, cash comes out, stock values increase or decrease, but the actual internal mechanism is not seen as important, even though this is where jobs are created. It is also where costs to society through such things as pollution and other forms of waste are generated but not fully met. If we don't understand businesses, and what motivates people in those businesses, then the economic superstructure runs the risk of being nonsense, as with the example of *Homo economicus*.

So what should we believe when it comes to economics if the established models do not work? What should we focus on instead?

Understanding our customers, who they are and what they desire from our product is key and has nothing to do with rational thinking. We must also accept that conventional approaches to business – such as making a business plan, finding investors, aiming to exit the company and retire – often don't work either. A far wiser strategy is to have a mitigation plan to reduce the risk of the business failing in the first place.

Another model that's gaining more traction is experimenting with innovation. It's described in a book by Eric Ries called *The Lean Startup*, and I examine this in depth in Chapter 11 on innovation.

The point is that endless growth for the sake of it ultimately doesn't serve people and is gradually killing our planet. Growing capitalist economies are destroying the natural world with deforestation, ever-growing carbon emissions and endless consumption of natural resources. All of this contributes to global warming, which impacts weather systems, causing the increasing occurrence of destructive floods, heatwaves and famines.

Most scientists believe the Earth's temperature is dangerously close to a tipping point where complete breakdown will inevitably occur. Time is not on our side – this is a global emergency.

When it comes to starting a new business, then, the climate issue must be at the forefront. Prioritizing the environment is giving rise to a new breed of eco-entrepreneurs: businesspeople who choose to minimize their impact on the natural world.

The national discourse on... GDP

Gross domestic product (GDP), based on the value of goods and services during a given period, is the main measure of growth in the UK.

How many times have you heard how important GDP growth is for a healthy economy? Or that it is a measure of the national wealth and therefore well-being? But this archetypal model of the nation's success is also flawed.

GDP focuses on financial growth only, excluding many factors which really matter to people and that affect our day-to-day quality of life – the factors that truly provide worthwhile wealth.

These include life expectancy, equal opportunities, environment, literacy rates, disease rates and unpaid contributions to the economy, such as caring roles and domestic roles. GDP also doesn't account for environmental damage, reduction in leisure time, depletion of non-renewable natural resources and depreciation of fixed assets.

The US senator Robert F. Kennedy said in 1968 that GDP 'measures everything… except that which makes life worthwhile'.[11] How right he was.

*

In her groundbreaking book *Doughnut Economics,* Oxford University academic Kate Raworth highlights the potentially disastrous consequences of untamed growth when issues such as damage to the environment are ignored.

---

[11] Robert F. Kennedy, Remarks at the University of Kansas, March 18, 1968, *John F. Kennedy Presidential Library and Museum,* www.jfklibrary.org/learn/about-jfk/the-kennedy-family/robert-f-kennedy/robert-f-kennedy-speeches/remarks-at-the-university-of-kansas-march-18-1968 (accessed 10 March 2024).

Raworth identifies seven major ways we could think differently about the economic system, and she advocates a new road map for change. The 'doughnut' represents two rings: the inner ring is the social foundation, which ensures citizens do not fall short on life's essentials, such as food, shelter and education, as well as providing value and purpose to allow people to flourish; the outer ring is the ecological ceiling, which must be in place to protect the Earth's supporting systems. Within these two rings of the doughnut is the safe space of 'dynamic balance', where all our social needs can be met without harming the environment.

Raworth argues that we need to rethink old economic models and meet the challenges of this century with bold approaches before the planet is destroyed. Growth simply cannot be endless. Figures prove that as GDP grows so too does air and water pollution.

Raworth notes that, in the 1930s, the US government asked an economist, Simon Kuznets, to work out how to measure national income and he came up first with the measure of gross national product, and later GDP.

But, interestingly, three decades later, Kuznets himself became cynical about his own model, pointing out that it only revealed part of a nation's wealth, namely market performance, omitting other equally important values.

What is the answer? Hopefully, change is coming in the form of groundbreaking ideas, including ditching the old GDP model. In 2019, then New Zealand Prime Minister Jacinda Ardern announced a progressive policy which would ditch the GDP measure to focus on the well-being of citizens instead. *'Economic growth accompanied by worsening social outcomes is not success… It is failure,'* she said.[12]

Since then, Finland, Iceland, Scotland and Wales have all become members of the Wellbeing Economy Governments partnership. Their aim is to transform economies around the world to deliver shared well-being for people and the planet by 2040. The UK government is yet to catch up, but it must place this idea on the agenda.

I believe small business is key for driving change in society. Small businesses have the flexibility to meet new market demands and make speedy changes. The Covid-19 crisis proved this. One study by Goldman Sachs, published in 2022, quizzed 1,000 of their alumni and found that during the pandemic, the majority (68%) were able to change their business models and many increased turnover.[13]

Small business is also driving forward the sustainability agenda, with 81% saying social and environmental factors influence their daily decision-making.[14]

An ethical business ethos must be front of mind when considering your start-up. How can your start-up idea be sustainable? What parts of your business will serve the well-

---

[12] Joe McCarthy, Jacinda Ardern says economic growth is pointless if people aren't thriving, *Global Citizen* (25 September 2019), www.globalcitizen.org/en/content/jacinda-ardern-goalkeepers-unga-2019 (accessed 19 March 2024).

[13] How small businesses are driving UK growth, *Goldman Sachs* (27 January 2022), www.goldmansachs.com/intelligence/pages/from-briefings-27-january-2022.html (accessed 19 March 2024).

[14] How small businesses are driving UK growth, *Goldman Sachs*.

being of others? What values can you as an individual bring to the business?

The traditional values of GDP and growth can and must be overtaken by better values for all.

Bob's musings from a mountain top

Many of the issues I have raised in relation to individuals and businesses around the need for a wider definition of wealth which encompasses all aspects of well-being are encapsulated in Raworth's *Doughnut Economics*.

Broadly speaking, a narrow focus on profits and shareholders at the individual and business levels translates into a narrow focus on GDP and growth at the macroeconomic level.

A key aspect of the doughnut discussion is that the economy is a complex, adaptive system. A basic feature of such systems is that they cannot be planned, but rather must evolve, usually because of a large number of innovative experiments undertaken by individuals and individual businesses, some of which will succeed and some of which will not.

Raworth refers to *The Origin of Wealth* by Eric Beinhocker, who championed this approach, and inspired my own approach to innovation. It is also the basis of the lean and agile approaches that have been widely and successfully adopted in the manufacturing and software worlds. The important point here is that the ideas introduced by Raworth are best addressed – and, indeed, can only be addressed –

from the ground up, starting at the individual and business levels rather than from the macro level.

The problem with starting at the macroeconomic level is that the political and financial worlds cannot react to ideas for a thriving economy that are put forward at grassroots level. Inhabitants of this world are addicted to the ideas of top-down planning, growth and GDP even though, on their own, these are not good enough measures of a nation's 'health'. Well-being depends on much more than just money; it incorporates environmental damage, reduction in leisure time, depletion of non-renewable natural resources and depreciation of fixed assets. In fact, if just one of these factors were to be included – the cost of environmental damage, for example – GDP would be significantly less than the figures currently published.

This thinking casts a new light on the importance of the individual and the role of small businesses in a nation's well-being. It is the best starting point and, indeed, the one best fitted to Raworth's 'doughnut' framework. The political and financial worlds (the old world) will be the last to adapt to doughnut economics, and starting at the business level, these new approaches – for which this book aims to provide inspiration – will emerge and evolve whether the old world likes it or not.

In essence, the world of evolutionary economic development will replace the world of top-down economic decision-making. The job of the entrepreneur is to ensure that individual well-being and the importance of all aspects of wealth (not just having money) play a full part in this evolutionary process.

A bottom-up approach appeals both to people's idealism and their self-interest in wanting to enjoy a balanced and fulfilling lifestyle. If we can inspire people to act by setting out ways in which individuals can take more control over their work life, then we will be contributing to this process.

The national discourse on... class and hierarchy

Social hierarchy is an established and accepted order, but one that everyone should challenge. UK society is obsessed with class, and people are quick to pigeonhole themselves and others within this hierarchy. We look at what we – and our parents, our friends and our neighbours – do for a living and often conclude: 'This is my lot in life.' But challenging the status quo, especially if you missed opportunities through education, can feel insurmountable.

But just because hierarchy and class run deep in the national psyche doesn't meant people can't drastically improve their lives and, indeed, create worthwhile wealth in spite of it.

Here's a social class hierarchy that's not really changed for hundreds of years:

1. **Individuals with inherited wealth.** This refers to people with huge inherited wealth who do not need to work for money and can do whatever they wish.
2. **Professionals.** This refers to high-paid workers with high levels of education and high-level skills. Examples include city types working in finance and professionals such as doctors, lawyers and accountants.

3. **Skilled workers.** This refers to workers who have specialized training. They may work in non-manual or manual occupations.
4. **Unskilled workers.** This refers to workers with no specialized training. However, the term is desultory and wrong. Every single job involves some level of skill. Try working as a waiter (as I have done) and it'll soon become obvious!

The hierarchy reflected in this list is based on an outrageously snobbish attitude which still persists today and has an unhealthy impact on the economy and society in general. I believe all can aspire to live at the top of the list, at least in terms of choosing what we do day to day, and you don't need to marry an aristocrat to do so. We all have the opportunity to pursue our interests AND be productive in the widest sense of the word (i.e. not only financially) if we are willing to break free of the career tramlines. Becoming an entrepreneur is one way of doing this.

The national discourse on... business stereotypes

Recently I watched *The Apprentice* on TV and thought: *'Goodness me, I couldn't win an episode on this, let alone the series!'*

The contestants were mostly loud-mouthed people focusing on the aggressive 'sell, sell, sell' at all costs attitude rather than practising strategic thinking. It's great TV, but the show got me thinking too. It's time to confront these cultural stereotypes of who is an entrepreneur and what makes a business successful.

The media portrayal of entrepreneurs is of shark-eyed profiteers who climb up the greasy pole, stepping on others' heads along the way. Once they reach the top of their game, they then spend their money on luxurious items to show the world how far they have come. Status and ego are coveted. Values and contentment, and freedom to be who you are, far less so.

Not only is it enough to put anyone off trying, it's not even an accurate portrayal of how business actually works. Almost everyone I know who succeeds in business is affable, smart, level-headed, ethical and trustworthy. They must be, otherwise their business wouldn't survive.

Recently I set up the Entrepreneurs' Forum, which invites entrepreneurs from all backgrounds to meet up, network, chat, help each other with problems and discuss ideas. From the beginning, it really struck me how down to earth this bunch were, how diffident and lacking in ego they seemed – the complete opposite to what happens when managers come together, with egos revealed very fast.

In our Entrepreneurs' Forum, the entrepreneurs are all quietly focusing on their objectives.

They are open-minded folk who listen deeply because they want to learn. They are in this to push their business or product forward and solve problems, rather than push themselves forward.

For this book, I have spoken to many who became accidental entrepreneurs. Entrepreneurs don't always need to see themselves as 'businesspeople' and do not need to conform to stereotypes. Many people possess natural skill sets, especially when it comes to pursuing something they feel a passion for.

The national discourse on... the critics

> Here's my advice. The first step to becoming a changemaker... is to give oneself permission, i.e. to ignore – politely, of course – all those who say: 'Don't do it!'
>
> —Bill Drayton[15]

Whatever you set out to do, you will come across people who will tell you: *'No, you can't do that.'* This might sound terribly cynical, but it's part of our national discourse to be critical of others' attempts at doing something different.

I've come up against so many middle managers or people in the public sector or in finance whose automatic response is to say 'No!' that I've come to expect it. Regardless of whether the idea was good or bad, there are many people who simply don't like new ideas.

There are also the malign observers out there, who like to sit back and watch when someone is trying something (especially something different) with unwanted commentary like:

---

[15] Bill Drayton, Best advice: don't follow it! *LinkedIn* (26 February, 2013), www.linkedin.com/pulse/20130226120357-119256144-best-advice-don-t-follow-it (accessed 19 March 2024).

'What are you doing that for?'

'If I were you, I'd do [insert something completely different].'

'You think that'll sell, do you?'

'I can't see that working.'

At one point or another, each of the above has been said to me, often at tricky times, so brace yourself! I always felt like saying something like 'Well, *you aren't doing it are you?*', but in the main I kept my mouth shut.

Why do people do this? I think it's fear. Thinking outside of the box is something that people fear doing themselves, so they see fit to criticize others. Expecting this discourse can help make ignoring it easier.

The national discourse on... status

Most of us don't get ascribed status at birth, because we're not born into aristocracy or royalty. Therefore, achieving a professional status is seen as a big accomplishment. Sought-after careers under the professional class umbrella include being a solicitor, doctor, banker, lawyer and financier – the type of career any middle-class parent traditionally aspires to for their kid.

These careers provide supposed lifelong security (although this is becoming rarer), respect and stability. And no doubt some of them can be immensely rewarding. Often, however, they are not.

Many doctors in the UK actively discourage others from going into the profession. A recent poll published in the *BMJ* revealed that 79% of junior doctors often think about leaving the National Health Service.[16]

Meanwhile, a survey of 3,000 young lawyers (aged 40 or below) revealed more than half were likely to move job and one in five had considered leaving the professions altogether.[17] The ongoing strikes across the public sector at this time are a sign the system no longer works either for the employees or those they are supposed to be serving – status or no status.

My wife was a GP and all four of my children are engineers, so I am well versed in what these professions involve, both positively and negatively, status-wise. Questioning what status certain jobs bring us is key in exploring what worthwhile wealth means to us. If a job that gives us status makes us unhappy, how valuable is it?

*

What happens if status is lost? How do we feel if we give up the 'safe' profession to try something different? This is one common fear that prevents people from setting up their dream business.

I experienced a perceived loss of status – totally unjustifiable – when I ditched a high-flying academic career to become

---

[16] Mathew R. Rammya, Why are doctors so unhappy? *BMJ,* 368: m100 (2020), www.bmj.com/content/368/bmj.m100 (accessed 19 March 2024).

[17] Significant numbers of young lawyers want to leave job, *LawCare,* www.lawcare.org.uk/latest-news/significant-numbers-of-young-lawyers-want-to-leave-job (accessed 19 March 2024).

a teacher. But in my experience, loss of status only takes around a fortnight to recover from (and the same applies to gaining status!). We are all more adaptable and resilient than we think we are.

The roots of our attachment to status often come from what other people think of us. People end up in careers to please parents or find a sense of belonging in society without questioning if it's really what they want to do in life.

Case study: tales from a mountain top

When Peter Mills left university, he decided to train to be a solicitor in pursuit of a career he believed would be worthwhile. Years later, he realized life as a lawyer wasn't going to bring him the contentment he'd been striving for…

When I left school for university, like many of my peers, I bought into the message that only successful people went to university and landed corporate-style jobs. It was the time of the Blair government and 'education, education, education' was the very much the national discourse at the time.

My family ran a successful fish and chip shop, but at the time the culture was to follow further education wherever possible, as this was viewed as a pathway to success.

So, I trained as a solicitor and worked in law for a decade. I believed the law industry would bring me a sense of purpose, status and the feeling of success I longed for.

However, years after qualifying, I realized it took at least 20 years of hard graft in the job before people considered you to be 'experienced'. I didn't feel prepared to sacrifice the long hours needed to devote to a job I didn't find very fulfilling, so ended up quitting. Depending on who I speak to, I am either a lawyer who saw the light or a failed solicitor!

I made the decision to retrain and set up a small digital agency, using computer and marketing skills. Eventually, I sold the business in 2020 in order to set up Crysp Ltd, a Bradford-based digital platform that specializes in helping companies navigate health and safety issues. I find this role hugely rewarding work, as I am helping small businesses achieve their goals and navigate legal obligations to be a success.

My company fits around my personal life too, as I have a young family and want flexible working hours to spend time with them.

It has been said the UK is a nation of 'small shopkeepers', and this was viewed in a derogatory way for a long time. But life has moved on. Many of my peers, now also in their mid-life, also feel cheated by their pursuit of big professional careers, so the idea of running a small business is extremely appealing.

The promise of a stable 'professional' career with status didn't bring any of them the satisfaction they thought it would either. Now there is no need to be embarrassed about trying a start-up or working for yourself or a family-run business. It's about making personal choices to suit your needs.

Further reading

Kate Raworth, *Doughnut Economics: Seven Ways to Think Like a 21st-Century Economist* (2016).

Tim Jackson, *Prosperity Without Growth: Economics for a Finite Planet* (2009).

Cath Bishop, *The Long Win: The Search for a Better Way to Succeed* (2020).

Eric Beinhocker, *The Origin of Wealth: Evolution, Complexity, and the Radical Remaking of Economics* (2006).

4

The positive impact of entrepreneurism

In this chapter, I examine:

- Why society needs more entrepreneurs
- The positive ripples small businesses create
- Types of entrepreneur

Entrepreneurship is living a few years of your life like most people won't so you can spend the rest of your life like most people can't.
—Warren G. Tracy's student

In *Doughnut Economics*, Kate Raworth says: 'Today we have economies that need to grow, whether or not they make us thrive; what we need are economies that make us thrive, whether or not they grow.' And I couldn't agree more.

Businesses that flourish have long-term strategies that create positive ripple effects in the wider community, and it's entrepreneurs who can create these conditions. Entrepreneurs drive the improvement of technologies, products and services. They promote social change and encourage a positive culture embracing innovation and respect for customers, and they are willing to break with tradition and pioneer new systems. Their businesses can be big or small, growing or not growing, and still create worthwhile wealth.

So many of us are ready for this change, especially young people or those of us who are disillusioned with the private sector grind. Going to university was once a pathway most academically capable students happily followed, but today graduates face debts of £60,000 that will take a lifetime to pay back. Many end up wanting to change career too, feeling burnt out and disillusioned by the time they reach middle age in professions that give a regular pay cheque and stability but little else.

Entrepreneurism has become more accessible to everyone thanks to the internet. Online, we can find tools, resources and insights into how other entrepreneurs have succeeded – we have access to a wealth of information previous generations could only dream of. In addition, new markets have been made possible by digital technology, including e-commerce. Indeed, entire business operations can be researched, set up and operated online. Via social media, a business can be marketed and a following created within weeks.

Entire supportive business communities exist online too. Not that I advocate only operating online, as face-to-face relationships cannot be beaten, but almost every business these days needs a strong online presence with a professional website with information that consumers can easily navigate.

With this shared information, more people are realizing there is another way to make work work for them.

Entrepreneurs matter

Entrepreneurs are the life blood of our economy. In 2023, there were 5.55 million businesses in the UK, around 2 million more than at the turn of the century.[18] More and more people want to run businesses themselves and for very good reasons, many linked to seeking worthwhile wealth. With so many advantages and the potential to feel professionally fulfilled, it's no surprise that 64% of working-age people say they have seriously thought about starting their own business.[19]

Why do we *need* more entrepreneurs?

> My powers are ordinary. Only my application brings me success.
>
> —Isaac Newton

To answer the question of why we need more entrepreneurs, quite simply, it's because entrepreneurs get things done. They are not constrained by red tape like many company employees and managers. Entrepreneurs challenge the status quo; they breathe passion and life into problem-solving products and are in a strong position to propel society forwards.

---

[18] D. Clark, Business enterprises in the UK – statistics and facts, *Statista* (20 December 2023), www.statista.com/topics/6848/businesses-in-the-uk/#topicOverview (accessed 19 March 2024).

[19] Aaryaman Aashind, Entrepreneurship statistics UK edition [2024], *Cybercrew* (9 February 2024), https://cybercrew.uk/blog/entrepreneurship-statistics-uk/ (accessed 19 March 2024).

Very quickly, with little or no experience, an entrepreneur can create a business from nothing and become an integral part of an industry or community. I don't mean to make this sound easy, as it's far from that, but I do believe with the right mindset anything is possible.

Think of the entrepreneurs who have been 'disruptive'. Disruptive entrepreneurs shake up traditional business models or spot untapped markets, presenting a challenge to industry norms.

Elon Musk, for example, has transformed the electric car industry, and not in the way many people think either. It isn't his electric vehicles that captured the market so much as his efficient car charging systems, and that's why the electric vehicle uptake has been so huge.

The legendary Steve Jobs was a disruptive entrepreneur who created groundbreaking products and arguably changed the landscape of personal technology.

'The people who are crazy enough to think they can change the world are the ones who do' – this was the tag line from Apple's 'Think Different' commercial in 1997.[20] They created an emotive connection with their customers, vowing openly to make products that disrupt the computer industry – simple, small products that anyone could use. They went on to disrupt the music industry with the advent of the iPod, capturing the consumer's imagination again in a way no other MP3 player managed to do at the time.

---

[20] Walter Isaacson, The real leadership lessons of Steve Jobs, *Harvard Business Review* (2012), https://hbr.org/2012/04/the-real-leadership-lessons-of-steve-jobs (accessed 19 March 2024).

Another company I deeply admire is Siemens, the engineering and manufacturing company whose clear mission is to be carbon neutral in their operations by 2030. No doubt this journey will involve huge innovation and revolutionary products and services along the way in the post-hydrocarbon world.

More locally, in Yorkshire, we have the fantastic Bettys & Taylors, which is well known for Yorkshire Tea and the wonderful Bettys tea rooms. It was founded by a Swiss baker, Fritz Bützer (who later changed his name to Frederick Belmont), who established the first Bettys tearoom in Harrogate in 1919. The company is remarkable for its relentless focus on quality and attention to detail, and our local cafe in Ilkley is a daily reminder that this kind of approach will always attract customers if it is done well.

I believe we are on the upward tick of this trajectory of change, and over the next few decades the pace will increase exponentially. There has never been a more exciting time to become an entrepreneur.

The ripple effect of local business

Building a local business is like throwing a stone into a pond, often creating a positive ripple effect wherever it lands, especially in local communities. This is something consumers find appealing. People want to buy from businesses who care or who are helping to support others. Worthwhile wealth lies in the creation of these deeper, meaningful, socially responsible bonds.

Can you think of a local business with an appalling reputation? I doubt it, because local businesses like this simply cannot last. They need a solid reputation of being trustworthy for people to part with their money. (In Chapter 8, I explore what makes a business ethical.)

When a business is built locally, the founder gets to know local people and relationships soon develop. From these relationships, conversations build; often, improvements to the area are discussed and actioned, and civic affairs can be affected favourably.

The local economy benefits because these businesses tend to employ local people and use local services like accountants, lawyers, food shops and suppliers.

When I first started BTL Publishing, we looked to build offices on the site of a disused building overlooking the Leeds and Liverpool Canal. At first, when I suggested the idea of rebuilding the dilapidated former abattoir, I faced the usual blank faces from council officials (and there was me thinking they'd jump at the chance!).

The process of applying to take over the building to create office space was a big lesson in perseverance, but months later we managed to get the contract. Once building works began, an architect we were working with decided to move in too, which in turn inspired an insurance broker to do the same. Then, one day, a local lady came into the new office at lunchtime to sell us sandwiches. Soon, she was selling so many that she could afford a small premises across the road, which came to serve all the staff from the offices in the area. The positive ripple effect of the BTL office widened with every passing year.

Before long, the whole area transformed from a derelict, disused canal side into a thriving community, highly developed, teeming with flourishing businesses.

Boosting income to a local area isn't only about money. It also brings worthwhile wealth. For example, if a local person has a local job, they save time on their commute. They might be able to walk or take public transport to work, which is better for the environment. They'll make friendships and join local networks, which brings a further sense of connection and well-being.

Types of entrepreneur

Just as there are different types of people in general, motivated by different things, there are different types of entrepreneur. Consider the following descriptions, which may help you decide what entrepreneur type best suits your character and potential business idea.

- **The start-up entrepreneur** – possibly the most common type, this is someone who starts a small business from scratch. A scalable start-up is a business that grows rapidly and quickly. Most are ideas or technology based or market led.
- **The social entrepreneur** – someone who starts a business with a specific cause in mind and with the aim of creating lasting social change. Whether operating locally or globally, these people are often change-makers with a deep sense of empathy. Bill Drayton is considered one of the first social entrepreneurs (and he coined the phrase), and his

company, Ashoka, went on to fund 3,000 change-makers in more than 70 countries.

- **The innovative entrepreneur** – someone who creates something completely new or pushes forward an existing technology to expand or develop it to make it profitable. Extra challenges include the possibility of being too early or late to the market. The market might need educating before your product arrives, and often it involves several iterations. Steve Jobs, who revolutionized phone and computer tech, and Jeff Bezos, who changed the face of e-commerce, are two of the best-known innovators.

- **The hustler** – someone who goes out and gets the sales. Alan Sugar is an example. The term 'hustler' conjures up the image of a risk-taking, aggressive salesperson, but another word to describe this sort of person is passionate. Money is often a central driving factor. Hustlers can be good at identifying and resolving short-term problems and have persuasive communication and sales skills.

- **The imitator** – someone who identifies a product or service that already works and tries to revolutionize and advance the idea. Arguably, if the market exists already for the product, this route can be easier compared to the path of the innovator, who must first educate the market. A famous imitator is Mark Zuckerberg, co-founder of Facebook. He started the company in his dorm room, as a 19-year-old computer science student, by copying and improving on existing social media tech.

- **The opportunist** – a reactive form of entrepreneurship, this is someone who spots and seizes on an opportunity as it arises in the market, rather than creating something new. It could be someone who has worked in a market for years and identified a pain point. In other instances, the entrepreneurship is a pure accident. One famous example is Arthur Fry, a scientist at the highly innovative company 3M. He was chatting to a fellow researcher who mentioned coming across a weak but reusable glue and wondered whether a product could be made from it. Fry tried the idea on paper, first using it as a bookmark, and then developed it into what would become the Post-it note. That opportunity led to sales worth billions worldwide and a product that has become a household name.

Broadly speaking, all entrepreneurs also fall into two distinct categories:

- **Market led** – someone who has experience in the field, spots a gap in the market and then uses their skills to try something new, usually modifying existing products or services. Most people who set up a business later in life are market led. They may have worked in the industry for several years and decide to go it alone. They have responsibilities – mortgages, families, spiralling cost of living expenses – and so might keep hold of their existing jobs while they set up their new business.
- **Technology or ideas led** – these entrepreneurs tend to be younger than those who are market led. Starting

up a business in this field is higher risk, as the market may not be ready. It can also take longer to develop and grow the business. Therefore, it is even more imperative to develop ways to mitigate the risk, such as managing variable costs.

*

The experience of trying, failing, facing the challenges and finding the right path for you is what sorts the dreamers from the doers. As author and inspirational speaker Simon Sinek says: 'Dream big. Start small. But most of all start.'

Further reading

Ollie Henderson, *Work/Life Flywheel: Harness the Work Revolution and Reimagine Your Career Without Fear* (2023).

Charles Handy, *The Age of Unreason* (1989).

5

Limbering up to start up

In this chapter, I examine:

- The doubts every new start-up founder faces
- What FEAR really means
- The importance of mentors
- How to settle on a business idea

The journey of a thousand miles begins with a single step.

—Lao Tzu

I'm ready.

My hiking boots are weatherproofed, my laces tied firmly, my rucksack filled with snacks, my compass and map to hand. A group of walkers aged from 20 to 60 are milling around behind me, waiting for the word to set off.

I gaze up at the mountain, check the map again and... off we go!

On this particular walk, I am in Kinlochleven, Scotland, and face a ferret's nest of paths and footways as I try to find a way out of the village. Despite my preparation, there are still many decisions to make. Is that the right stile ahead, or should we take the narrower path by the church? Would that set of stony steps take us to the main route, or should we go the long way around, by a river?

I sense the trepidation of the walkers behind me as my footsteps slow. Although I see our objective, one of the Mamores, looming over us, my mind races with the myriad choices for how to get us there safely.

As leader, I need to decide. Despite being with friends, my credibility is up for question. Choose the wrong path and I could add an hour to our estimated journey time. In short, before even taking the first tentative steps, I am suddenly in fear of looking like a chump.

It's then I am struck by how similar setting off on a big walk is to taking those first steps with a new business venture.

Those first steps are the hardest part, especially when you know others are watching. It can lead to uncharacteristic procrastination, where you try to eliminate every potential risk before you've even begun.

It's this fear, especially when it's related to fear of losing face, that stops potential entrepreneurs in their tracks.

Starting a new business means becoming vulnerable, as things may not work out. The observer we think is watching us might just be our own internal critic. You know the one, the voice inside who asks:

'What if… [insert worst-case scenario]?'

'Who do you think you are?'

'*Will you make a mess of this?*'

'*How much financial loss could this lead to?*'

These questions trip us up, make us paranoid about making a mistake or deride us before we even step on the path we want to follow.

We all have this inner voice of doubt. How much we listen to it depends on our life experience, our upbringing and how conscious we are of deciding to overcome the fears in our head.

Popular excuses

For many, 'dreaming' is easier than 'doing', and coming up with a mile-long list of excuses for why you can't do something feels natural. Let's look at that list now. Common excuses centre around things we don't have, like:

- Time
- Money
- Experience
- Qualifications
- Head space

These can feel like very valid excuses. I can't offer sure-fire solutions to every reader's individual mental barrier. What I do know is this: any odds can be beaten. I did it myself and I have spoken to many others who have started businesses despite difficult or seemingly impossible environments.

But first we must confront our fear. Fear is what lies behind the many excuses we come up with. But I think of fear as **False Evidence Appearing Real (FEAR)**.

This way of looking at fear relates specifically to risks in business. Fear is a reaction to a threat. My reading of it, however, is that the only *real* threats are those that threaten death or physical injury. All other threats are secondary concerns and therefore are indeed False Evidence Appearing Real. The main fears every entrepreneur must face include:

- Fear of failure
- Fear of loss of status
- Fear of losing money

People may convince themselves that a business 'failure' would be a disaster, and one they would not recover from. In practice, we often make predictions that turn out to be wrong.

I see two main ways of challenging the fear of failure in a start-up.

First, do what you can to ensure any potential downsides are manageable for your business. I examine this in detail in Chapter 10 on risk mitigation. Foreseeing challenges and managing these risks is how you overcome them.

Second, be prepared to change your thought processes when something is not going to plan. Rather than seeing it as failure, end of, view it as an experiment and a learning opportunity. Constant innovation and flexibility lie at the heart of any successful business. I explore this in Chapter 11 on innovation.

Fear of change

This is the fear of unknown outcomes. People may believe that any change will result in negative consequences, even without any evidence to support this. Living with uncertainty, however, is an integral part of being an entrepreneur, and people can and do get used to it. I believe uncertainty is much easier to manage when you can accept it as normal rather than seeing it as a harbinger of doom.

In my business life, whenever I have been faced with FEAR – usually associated with the possibility of money running out – I have eased the mental process by thinking to myself: *'Nothing was ever achieved without one leg over the precipice.'*

This saying makes me smile inwardly and reduces the immediate feeling of the fear. Sitting in a comfort zone is where we find predictability, so-called stability, but is not where we learn or develop as human beings. Learning to feel comfortable being 'uncomfortable' is an emotion every new entrepreneur must be prepared for.

Remember, threats you face as an entrepreneur nearly always create FEAR rather than real fear.

Case study: tales from a mountain top

Jo Thornley was a French teacher for many years before deciding to improve her work–life balance by setting up a one-woman plumbing business. She did supply teaching and exam invigilating to pay bills as she returned to college to retrain…

Teaching was a harder profession once it became a box-ticking exercise, and I no longer enjoyed the job at all because of the all extra paperwork.

I had always secretly wondered what it would be like to be a plumber. The idea of working for myself, doing something with my hands and providing a useful service was highly appealing. I couldn't afford to give up work completely, so took on supply teaching and other work to pay for the bills then took the plunge and joined NVQ Level 2 and 3 plumbing courses to retrain.

I was the only woman on the courses and my young male classmates made jokes about their mother coming along to study, but I had a lot of motivation to do this and laughed along with them.

After qualifying, I chose to work alongside other established plumbers at first, to pick up further tips and skills of how to run a successful business. Watching how others did this was invaluable; it boosted my confidence as I observed how to deal with real-life experiences on the job.

I also found funding with a grant to complete a short business course, which explained how to market and brand a new company to attract as many customers as possible.

Then, I set up my own company, working under my name 'Jo' so people didn't necessarily know I was a female plumber. Only once did a customer criticize my work, standing over me as I tried to fix her taps, so I had to stand up for myself. But overall, although people were surprised to see a woman, they were perfectly fine and happy with my work.

Marketing wasn't something I needed to pursue, as most of my work came from word of mouth from happy customers. On occasion, I couldn't manage to lift the heavy equipment, so I took on a young apprentice. He was so keen, I decided to help pay for him through his official training. He flourished into a talented plumber who now runs his own successful business. That's one of my most satisfying achievements.

Looking back, I took a big risk starting a new business in a completely new field later in life, but I wouldn't change a thing.

Being adaptable

It is not the strongest of the species that survives, nor the most intelligent that survives. It is the one that is most adaptable to change.[21]

---

[21] While this quotation is often attributed to Charles Darwin, there is some debate as to its origin – see the Darwin Correspondence Project at: www.darwinproject.ac.uk/evolution-misquotation (accessed 25 March 2024).

There will always be obstacles when setting up and running a business, but by being adaptable and recognizing that change is bound to happen, those obstacles can be overcome and may even lead to opportunities.

Case study: tales from a mountain top

Vanessa Ruddock started her cleaning company without any capital or experience, and as a single parent she had very little spare time. Her motivation stemmed from wanting employment that fitted in with her young family and wanting to give her children a better standard of living. She hasn't looked back since…

My advice to people is not to focus on what you can't do; focus on what you can do. Even if you have no time or money, just allocate what you can to the cause. Even an hour a day can go a long way. Imagine what could be achieved with months of persistence – it quickly builds up.

'Only look at the first step not the whole staircase' is one of my favourite phrases, because it helps eliminate the fear of beginning. Breaking down steps one at a time helps to keep you motivated. We all have self-limiting beliefs. Identify what yours are and confront them. I decided to write down positive affirmations to counteract my limiting beliefs and repeat them every day to myself.

My business began when I worked part time in a gym but needed extra income, so I asked around our customers about a cleaning job. Within weeks, I had so many clients I'd matched my gym wage, so roped in friends to help. A few months later, I had two part-time cleaners join me, and they asked to go on payroll, so I delegated this to an accountant.

I had no overheads and no need to advertise, because it was all word of mouth. However, to give the business a sense of legitimacy if people asked for online details, I set up a Facebook page and small website, calling the business Purely Polished.

I always felt ambitious and began to see potential from what I was creating. I could work my hours around my young children, making sure I was always there to do the school pick-ups and drop-offs and not have to work in the evenings. I longed to be there for them, give them holidays and pay for a decent lifestyle.

I employed other women who also wanted to work around family time, and so I made the decision to work with my staff and not against them. I wanted to be flexible for them and in turn they became loyal to me. I faced challenges on the way, including learning how to manage people, but I kept trying to keep a positive mindset, even repeating mantras when I woke up in the morning to keep my head in a good space. I had to learn fast every day but tried to view failures as learning curves.

Things just grew and grew. We got an enquiry from a local business to do their office. I had no idea if this was possible, due to the size of the job, but I immediately said yes to it. With help and others pitching in, we got the job done.

After a year, I had 3 employees, and after five years, I had 12. Half our contracts came from businesses and half from domestic jobs.

Recently, I decided to sell the business, as I want to focus on helping other people with their small business start-ups. My journey proved to me that anything is possible, and it's time for me to help others with their dreams.

Further reading

Jo Richardson, *Ignite: Bring Your Business to Life Without Burning Out* (2021).

6

Before the big leap: understanding the 'why' of your business

In this chapter, I examine:

- The importance of understanding the 'why' behind your start-up
- How the 'why' of a business can evolve
- How to communicate the 'why'

Part of limbering up before launching a new business involves identifying the reasons for setting it up in the first place. Before leaping to launch, you must fully understand and get behind *why* your business needs to exist at all.

Ideally, any start-up founder should be able to shout their key message in one single sentence from the top of a mountain so that everyone can understand why their product or service is needed.

The big 'why'

Your business needs to solve a problem, address a particular pain point or create an aspiration. Aspiration can be a harder sell, but that's another book in itself.

Being clear about the 'why' in your own mind makes it easier to communicate the value of your business to other people – your customers, potential investors or mentors. It makes your branding and marketing easier too.

But, most importantly, having a 'why' gives YOU a reason for doing this. It's why you get out of bed in the morning, and it brings a definite sense of purpose and value to your work and efforts. If you don't know why you're doing something, then why would you or anyone else care? Not having a 'why' for your work creates frustration, confusion and often burnout.

Worthwhile wealth means finding a job that creates a raison d'être rather than simply being a money-making exercise.

The 'why' doesn't have to be especially fancy or noble. It could be as simple as wanting to make the tastiest cakes in your village or to knit the warmest woolly hats for children. Of course, some people do simply want to make lots of money, but it is very hard to sustain motivation on that basis alone, and customers can sense whether you have a passion for your business and a strong underlying message or whether you're just phoning it in.

HF Holidays has been successful for over 110 years on the basis of a simple initial set of 'whys' – the healthy enjoyment of leisure, love of the open air and the promotion of social and international friendship. The words have changed over the years, but this basic message has underpinned all its activities.

As Simon Sinek says: 'People don't buy what you do; people buy why you do it.'[22] The 'why' of your business is how people will connect with it in an emotive way. Businesses that flourish create a following or a community, or bring a sense of value into consumers' lives.

In his book *Start with Why*, Sinek shows that Apple is a brilliant example of this. Why did Apple succeed so hugely, while other tech companies released similar products at the same time and failed? Look at the Apple iPod versus the Dell MP3 player. It's because Apple had already given customers a clear sense of *why* they were creating their product, and they openly stated they were trying to disrupt the music industry and the way customers could access music.

Apple had created a loyal following of early adopters who couldn't live without their latest product, but they also appealed to a mass market because their marketing was far more emotive than anything Dell had created.

'Why' leads to a greater chance of success

It's more important to understand the 'why' question than the 'how' or 'what' questions when it comes to business, as Sinek explains in *Start with Why*:

Knowing your WHY is not only the way to be successful, but it is the only way to maintain a lasting success and have a greater blend of innovation and flexibility. When a WHY

---

[22] Simon Sinek, How great leaders inspire action [video], *TED* (2009), www.ted.com/talks/simon_sinek_how_great_leaders_inspire_action/transcript (accessed 19 March 2024).

goes fuzzy, it becomes much more difficult to maintain the growth, loyalty and inspiration that helped drive the original success.

Even big, established businesses can fail if they forget the answer to their 'why' question. Businesses that were once household names have fallen apart because they lost their sense of 'why', often when failing to innovate with fast-changing technology.

Toys R Us was once the go-to shop for toys, but fell apart after signing a deal with Amazon, having failed to innovate with e-commerce. Similarly, Borders bookshop didn't digitize fast enough and sales fell through the floor, and Kodak got overtaken by Canon for failing to embrace digital tech.[23]

Without consciously doing so, I decided on the 'why' of my businesses early on, and it really sustained both me and eventually my team to keep driving towards our bigger purpose.

The 'why' for my businesses was to dramatically improve education and healthcare through the judicious use of technology.

In 1992, I set up BTL Publishing because I had a clear vision about making learning equitable through the use of technology but couldn't find a publisher for my new e-learning material.

---

[23] Frances Goh, 10 companies that failed to innovate, resulting in business failure, *Collective Campus*, www.collectivecampus. io/blog/10-companies-that-were-too-slow-to-respond-to-change (accessed 19 March 2024).

Education and health technology is a very hard nut to crack; progression is always slow because these are government-controlled sectors and led from the top down. Thirty years on, despite many commercial successes, I still feel like I haven't achieved my overall goal, although I truly believe we're on the point of a breakthrough. Along the way, I have instead been involved in many innovations, including the founding of Virtual College, which brought computer-based learning (now called e-learning) to a worldwide vocational training market.

But the original 'why' still exists – it hasn't shifted since 1978. This 'why' has given me a solid set of values to stand by during incredibly tough times. It has also provided my staff with the bigger-picture reason for why they're getting up in the morning, coming to the office and slogging away. They have a true sense of purpose; we are delivering computer systems designed to make people's lives better.

When we set up ADI (Advanced Digital Institute and, later, Advanced Digital Innovation) in 2005 as a not-for-profit company, it had a clear 'why' from the start. It was to be a social enterprise to encourage tech innovations.

It was a deliberate model to encourage people from the academic sector with disruptive ideas to create start-ups in industry, especially in the health and technology sectors. Based in West Yorkshire, the vision was to engage with universities, innovators and people who have good ideas to help create companies that use technology for the good and encourage growth in our part of the world.

As John Eaglesham, former CEO of ADI, says: 'I have worked in stressful jobs previously but never had to drag myself out of bed in the morning to do this one. We all knew we were trying to achieve something purposeful, and working towards social purpose with life-changing results for people was thrilling.'

ADI success stories include:

- Helping a start-up by a young woman who was doing a PhD and wanted to set up a business using data analysis for MRI scans. This is now a very successful company.
- Helping to develop a video consultation service to enable specialist clinicians at Airedale General Hospital to talk to people at home. This technology is now used in hundreds of care homes across the UK.
- Creating an online platform to help children's mental health so that young people can seek help faster rather than sit for agonizing months on waiting lists.
- Developing groundbreaking online communication tools for people with motor neurone disease so that they can communicate their needs to specialists instantly. It means patients don't need to wait for appointments and travel for miles to get to specialist centres. This application was already in place prior to the lockdown of 2020 caused by the Covid-19 pandemic, and this proved to be vital, because it was possible to fast-track its use at this time.
- Our biggest success: the technology that led to MyPathway, a system allowing patients to track their appointments and doctors' feedback instead of relying on the antiquated method of letters and paperwork. All Sheffield hospitals currently use this pioneering system.

Discovering your 'why'

The 'why' for a business often stems from the shared values the founders have with people around them. The biggest influences in our lives are often family, friends, local communities and, sometimes, bigger-picture people, like social media influencers or public role models.

Entrepreneurs should take the following steps when deciding on their start-up 'why':

1. Write down five reasons why you want to start the company (e.g. because your product will make life easier for consumers; because the product is sustainably sourced).
2. Write down what values the company will care about (these might be ethical values or societal values).
3. Write down what goals emerge from these values (e.g. to create a more sustainable product than the nearest competitor).
4. Write down all the benefits from using the information above. Then, with this in mind, go through the steps again to really drill down into your 'why'.

To get to the heart of your 'why', you might use the '5 whys' technique developed in the 1930s by Sakichi Toyoda – the Japanese industrialist, inventor and founder of Toyota Industries Corporation – which became popular in the 1970s.[24]

---

[24] 5 whys, *Mind Tools*, www.mindtools.com/a3mi00v/5-whys (accessed 19 March 2024).

For example: Your business idea is to set up an ethical children's clothing company. You would answer a first 'why' question, then ask four further 'why' questions (to highlight the benefit of the previous why).

- Why? To create an online platform to encourage the recycling of kids' clothes.
- Why? To encourage parents to avoid fast fashion for their kids.
- Why? To avoid environmental waste with kids' clothes.
- Why? To save parents money in the long term.
- Why? To make decent clothes more affordable and environmentally friendly for more children.

And you don't have to stop at five 'why' questions...

- Why? To make fashion more equitable and environmentally friendly.

It's at this point a little research also goes a long way...

Doing research

> If we knew what it was we were doing, it would not be called research, would it?
>
> —Albert Einstein

When you are on the journey to discover your 'why', that's the time to research more deeply. There are two kinds of industry research: desk and field.

- **Desk research** is looking up data, surveys, sales figures, newspapers, trade press and anything you can lay your hands on that gives detailed research already carried out. It's a good way to grasp the overall market landscape and current and past trends. It's a relatively inexpensive, easy way to see the bigger picture of an industry, although be aware the information might be biased (e.g. if a certain company conducted the research and has a vested interest in the results) or it could be out of date.

- **Field research** is what scientists do outside the laboratory. It involves collecting the raw data, and can mean interacting with people (e.g. potential customers) and communities. This might involve informally chatting to people or collecting data in a more structured way – for example, via a structured interview or questionnaire. There are companies who can assist but this can be expensive as it takes up a lot of time and is labour-intensive. Depending on your potential business, however, the data could prove to be a goldmine of information.

Getting close to your potential customers and simply asking them why they want to buy the product can reap huge rewards. What are they looking for? How can what already exists in the market be improved on? What do they like and dislike about what is already available?

We often use this technique in our own business development. We ask our customers to put money towards a new development, offering them first chance to try it. Any investment really is a sign of true interest. I explore this further in Chapter 11 on innovation.

When the 'why' remains unclear

Sometimes at the beginning, however, the 'why' might not be straightforward. You might not be able to find your 'why' until you have done more experimentation – this can be true of both market- and tech/idea-led businesses.

Or it can be as simple as a personal reason making it harder to decide the scope of the business. For example, do you want to work from home, be laptop-based so you can work anywhere, or have bricks and mortar set-up?

It could be the groundbreaking idea you had needs tweaking because of a new trend, or the market might unexpectedly change so a new approach is necessary post launch. Sometimes, nailing the 'why' might have to wait until the start-up idea is more established and better understood.

Case study: tales from a mountain top

The 'why' for Rob Seal's business came through an evolutionary process. He decided to try out a completely new career in metal recycling after unexpectedly being made redundant from a corporate job. Eventually, he realized there was a gap in the market for recycling IT equipment and a service to secure data destruction that goes with that. The 'why' and brand emerged gradually, and today Ucan Secure IT is a multiple award-winning company based in Bradford...

I followed the path like many of my peers, going to university and studying a profession, which happened to be marketing. I thought I'd found my dream job working for a holiday company. I had a big salary, an assistant and first-class travel, until months later I was made redundant. I had two small children and thought: *'What do I do now!'*

My friend introduced me to a German metal trader who was looking for someone in the UK to source scrap metal and send it to Germany. I'd always enjoyed buying and selling, so despite not knowing anything about metals, I thought I'd try giving metal recycling a go.

It was a very steep learning curve, and I was grateful to have a mentor to ask many questions in the early days. I had no clue about any of the basics. The first job I managed to buy metal from was a large chemical site in Switzerland. I was staring at thousands of tonnes of pipes, tanks and cable and trying to estimate a value, knowing practically nothing about metal. This deal set me on my way and in 2009 I set up my first company, Seal Metal Recycling, from a friend's garage.

This felt like such a step down after my fancy job with my own PA and office, but I kept going to keep overheads to a minimum, because I enjoyed the sales side and found a passion for this new venture.

I quickly learned the basics and started visiting waste companies, buying tonnes and tonnes of aluminium cans – I used to get excited as rather than staring at piles of cans, in my mind I was staring at piles of cash.

The more I traded, the more I realized there was a niche market in recycling IT products. In fact, I realized this was a problem for businesses, that needed solving. What do companies do with all their old IT equipment? Especially when it has private data on it? Spotting a gap in the market, I decided to pivot and specialize in recycling IT products, guaranteeing a secure data removal service and putting the machines to good use again, stripping for parts or recycling.

I took on a lease of a small warehouse in Harehills, Leeds, and employed a bookkeeper and warehouse guys to help me collect, sort and recycle the IT parts.

The company grew to 12 people, and we started winning awards for recycling and job creation initiatives.

As the volumes of IT we were recycling grew year on year and we were financially stable, we took the plunge to lease a 30,000-square-foot warehouse in Bradford. We rebranded Ucan Secure IT Ltd and the business continues to grow.

Without having experimented in the market first, I would never have known to have created such a unique business. The 'why' has completely changed from the vision at the start; it's been a journey of discovery, but we've created a business to be proud of.

Further reading

Simon Sinek, *Start with Why: How Great Leaders Inspire People to Take Action* (2009).

7

Communicating the 'why'

In this chapter, I examine:

- The need for a clear brand identity
- The role of marketing

A brand for a company is like a reputation for a person.

—Jeff Bezos

Communicating your why is the next step. Deciding how this message is given to the customer is where the brand and marketing come into play. As early as possible, it's wise to consider the direction of the branding. Every single business needs to have a clear brand identity, including a name, logo and colours used across all their content, from letterheads to social media accounts.

The decisions made around the branding should reflect your 'why'.

Case study: tales from a mountain top

My friend Ian Thompson ran a brand agency for over three decades. He summarizes some of the main points to consider about branding here…

When we talk about 'brand', we're really talking about the sum of the thoughts and feelings a customer has about a company or a product. It can be made up of many things: how it looks, the way it projects itself, the service we get from it, the way it makes us feel – even something we've heard about it from someone else. It might even be an idea or a principle we associate with it. One way or another, a company's brand helps us make a connection with it, as if it's a person.

Customers often unconsciously ask themselves basic questions when they're considering whether to use a company:

- Do they feel professional/legitimate?

Some companies are happy to under-invest in their 'look' and 'feel' if they believe they have a good service or product. Sometimes they even imagine that branding is all just 'smoke and mirrors'. However, a company's 'look' and 'feel' are the first thing customers see, and we're all influenced by first impressions. Companies who underestimate this will never know how many potential sales they lost at this first hurdle. You should hope that your competitors take this view, because it's likely to contribute to their downfall.

If you believe you're the real thing, you should make sure you look like you are.

- Do they look like they'll still be around in years to come?

Even if a company only started this year, customers want to deal with companies that will last. It makes them feel safe. They want to feel like they've made the right choice. Look solid, dependable and up to date. Look like you're here for the long haul.

- Do they care about how they come across?

If a company makes it obvious that they don't really value the first impression they make, it forces the customer to ask themselves: '*What else don't they care about?*' Customers worry they might be taken for a ride. They want to believe in the company they're dealing with. So, take it seriously.

At the very least, the branding helps you compete with other businesses, but at best, it will guide the direction of your business. It can tell the customer the story of where you want to go in the future.

Here is my basic advice:

- Find out what's out there already.

This is not just about brand, it's about the whole business proposition. Have a look at what other businesses are doing in your sector/service area. Look particularly at the businesses who are at the top of the tree in your sphere of business. You'd be surprised how many businesses who've been around for 5 or even 10 years have never done this! They get so consumed by their big idea that they often fail to check if anyone else is doing precisely the same thing. Do some research on where others have been before, what they have done and how they've done it in order to make sure your business is genuinely differentiated.

Everything you discover will help to inform the direction of your business and your brand. Who are you? What's unique about you? This is something that comes up on the TV show *Dragons' Den* all the time. How often have we heard one of the dragons say: '*Hang on a minute, doesn't XYZ company already do this really well?*' And the camera pans around to capture the face of the contestant dropping like a stone.

- Work hard to get a decent name.

Most successful, standout brands have a great, memorable name. Some brands have such good names they barely need a logo. Your name should be easy to pronounce and, where possible, understandable. You could argue that Google is not understandable unless you know what it means, but it didn't matter in their case. It was the kind of name that once heard is never forgotten – Ask Jeeves didn't have a chance.

Sometimes new businesses choose a cool name as if they're choosing a name for a band! Of course, the name must work for you, but your customer is much more important than you. Always think about how it works for them.

Try to choose a name that will 'own' some territory for you. Don't shy away from making it simple – simple is usually best.

My company did some work for a new brewery owned by a friend of one of the account managers. The client came up with the name Anthology Brewing. It's a great name in a saturated marketplace, and it allowed him to keep coming up with new beers. It really hit the spot, and the name spawned the idea for how the brand should behave. We based all the beer labels on old book covers from the 60s and 70s. This is a brewer with real longevity who will create a library of different beers over the years! If the brewery had gone for something funky, it wouldn't really tell the customer much about the ethos of the company or the product.

Finally, companies get het up about securing the '.com' URL. It forces companies to come up with ridiculous names just to find something still available. Pretty much everything that makes any sense will have been gobbled up and offered for sale at extortionate prices. If you really must have the '.com' (though it's not the be all and end all in my opinion), add something to the beginning or end to make it unique. However, many companies are ignoring the '.com' for other suffixes. It's not what it used to be – you're still credible if you don't have a '.com' or a '.co.uk'. Don't let it result in a rubbish name for your company.

- It's not all about the logo.

Logos like those of Nike, McDonald's and Apple come along very rarely, but you'd be amazed how many times I've been asked to create something just as iconic for an accountancy firm or a solicitor. But it's still worthwhile to think about simple and clear design, what your logo should convey and what it should tell the customer about your business at a glance. Some huge brands like Starbucks and Mastercard have taken their name out of their logo, but that's only because their logos are so recognizable that their name is conjured straight away. You should bear in mind that your name itself could become your logo, but it's important you give the job to a designer. Don't try to do it yourself. It's not easy. Stick to running your business.

What you should be thinking about is your company's behaviour. What you do, how you conduct yourself and your view on the world is as much a part of your brand as anything else. And it's completely under your control.

Ian's words are spot on. I'd only add that if there is a product already in existence in the market, then it's not necessarily a disaster, because it already demonstrates there IS a market for it. Sometimes consumers feel suspicious of completely different products in a market, so again research is needed on what your business will add.

The marketing question

Marketing your product is the next step to communicating the why of your business.

Consider what kind of market research is needed. For a tech company, this will often be a waste of time, so instead consider the infamous 'P's of marketing too – the mix to engage customers, as made up by a Harvard Professor James Culliton in the 1948:

- **Product:** Clearly define the product and exactly what it offers the consumer. What problem does it solve or what does it offer to make them feel better? Note what the competitor's product is doing and what your product offers that is different. Defining the product will dictate cost and its place in the market.
- **Price:** Is your product aimed at the high end of the market as a luxury good, or at the lower end of the market as an everyday item? Ensure your price is reflective of the quality. Can you offer discounts to tempt new customers?

- **Place:** Once the product and price are decided, think about where your target consumers will find the product. Will you start by selling online only? Will you sell locally to begin with? Or should you find suppliers at a trade market? E-commerce has transformed the way business is done and any availability online is only likely to boost sales.
- **Promotion:** Place and promotion go hand in hand. This will involve a thoughtful strategy, ideally including advertising, use of SEO (search engine optimization) and Google ads for businesses, and basic public relations. Here, you might get advice from an expert or, better still, someone who has already set up a similar business successfully and can share their experience.

Inevitably marketing experts in the field have added more 'P's to the original four! These include:

- **People:** This is part of the promotion arm of the product. Who can market it? Use of social media influencers is on the rise, but decisions also need to be made as to the impact of the founder. As a founder, are you prepared to front your product to push sales? Evidence suggests consumers like to relate to the business owner. For example, if you have a personal reason for wanting to create your product, this adds to the 'why' of your business and creates a sense of authenticity. Are you prepared to be the face of your business if necessary?
- **Physicality:** This sounds odd, but in this world of online scams, there is a need to validate your product

and who you are. If there is no competitor out there, this can create suspicion about what this product is and who is behind it. A slick website offering an 'About' page, an introduction to the founder (or indeed a plotted story behind the company) and promises of prompt, secure delivery will help a new business gain trust. Stand by your words too – don't make promises that you can't deliver on.

- **Process:** Consider the logistics. Consumers always want fast, seamless delivery and a promise of satisfaction. How can you ensure this happens? Carefully select couriers or delivery services with proven track records. Make sure you can meet supply and demand.

Further reading

E. Jerome McCarthy, *Basic Marketing: A Managerial Approach* (1960).

Simon Sinek, *Find Your Why: A Practical Guide for Discovering Purpose for You and Your Team* (2016).

Ken Robinson, *The Element: How Finding Your Passion Changes Everything* (2008).

8

Building an ethical business

In this chapter, I examine:

- Why a business needs to be ethical to flourish
- The importance of reputation and transparency
- What good business ethics include

Culture is a thousand things, a thousand times. It's living the core values when you hire; when you write an email; when you are working on a project; when you are walking in the hall.

—Brian Chesky[25]

The word 'ethical' comes from the Greek *ethos*, meaning 'moral character', a person or behaviour that is 'right in the moral sense – truthful, fair, and honest'.[26]

---

[25] Brian Chesky, Don't f*uck up the culture, *LinkedIn* (24 April 2014), www.linkedin.com/pulse/20140424002919-13378252-don-t-f-ck-up-the-culture (accessed 10 March 2024).

[26] Ethical, *Vocabulary.com*, www.vocabulary.com/dictionary/ethical#: ~:text=Ethical%20comes%20from%20the%20Greek,moral%20 standards%20of%20their%20profession (accessed 25 March 2024).

On a walk in the countryside, it's easy to be ethical. Don't drop litter. Respect the pathways and boundaries and the flora and fauna. Close any gates you pass through. Be mindful of passers-by and by-laws.

In business, being ethical can also be viewed as straightforward. Be honest and open. Don't lie, don't cheat, but build a good reputation with suppliers, partners and customers alike. Essentially, bring the decent values we possess as human beings into our business values to create a culture to be proud of.

But for so many of us, ethics get compromised and we feel powerless to change this. Many decent people get stuck in jobs they don't believe in and don't want to do, and often they don't believe in the company values either. Fear of loss of finances or status overtakes concern about ethics. Working for corporations or industries we don't believe in is soul destroying but sadly normalized. Once again, the appeal of building a better way shines brightly.

The wider burden of poor ethics

Not only does poor ethics cause a burden on a personal level, but poor ethics in business creates a big burden on society – a price we all collectively pay, quite often with our taxes. In Chapter 3 on challenging national discourse, we saw how damaging outdated economic models are.

The continual obsession with growth at all costs means big corporations choose activity that is often at odds with employee values. It also leads to very risky borrowing when it is known someone else will have to pick up the pieces – for example, in the credit crunch, banks were bailed out using taxpayer money.

Similarly, the oil giants are not currently expected to pay for the damage created by the carbon dioxide (CO_2) emitted into the atmosphere as a result of use of their products, which leads to approximately 9% of global emissions.

When the UK water companies were privatized, they didn't have any debt, but now one of them has a debt of £14 billion,[27] and a similar pattern can be found in other water companies. A national debate is raging about whether this is due to poor regulation and big money being syphoned out to shareholders. Also, it is widely believed that they have a very poor record on releasing sewage into our waterways and beaches, killing thousands of fish and doing untold environmental damage.

Waste and pollution are not costed into companies' operations, leading to exaggerated profits. The water companies have been discharging sewage while at the same time paying large dividends to shareholders for many years, and governments have done nothing to stop this.

Despite the waste it entails, growth, in any guise, is still celebrated as a good thing. A bigger car, a bigger house, a longer holiday, a bigger bank balance... People rarely call into question this continual philosophy of having more for

---

[27] Harry Wise, Thames Water blames 'very low' bills for £14.7bn debt pile, *This Is Money* (13 December, 2023), www.thisismoney. co.uk/money/markets/article-12858845/Thames-Water-blames-low-bills-14-7bn-debt-pile.html (accessed 19 March 2024).

the sake of it, let alone question the impact on our climate. Bigger does not mean better.

However, growing a business isn't a bad idea, in fact many businesses need to grow to survive, but doing so should be purposeful and considered. Keeping close to the purpose will mean it is more likely be a success and not deviate from the ethics you started off with.

*

Back in 1994, sustainability thought leader John Elkington came up with the concept of the 'triple bottom line', referring to people, planet and profit – a business model to encourage integrity and ethical thinking rather than simply profit-making. More recently,[28] Elkington has expressed disappointment that this model has become a form of lip service for some companies. He would like to see more accountability, and this is a growing concern with consumers and employees alike.

Many giant companies have wonderfully ethical values formally emblazoned on their websites that bear absolutely no relationship to their products or day-to-day practices or company policies.

Scratch beneath the surface and many companies' ethical policies come undone, so deciding on what policies are

---

[28] John Elkington, 25 years ago I coined the phrase 'triple bottom line'. Here's why it's time to rethink it, *Harvard Business Review* (5 June 2018), https://hbr.org/2018/06/25-years-ago-i-coined-the-phrase-triple-bottom-line-heres-why-im-giving-up-on-it (accessed 19 March 2024).

realistic and sticking to them early on is a good idea. It's much harder to become ethical in retrospect.

What do we mean by an 'ethical' product or service?

Generally speaking, the 'ethical' side of a business looks at the human impact of the product, considering where and how it is sourced as well as how the company is run.

Key commitments for a start-up include:

- **Cause no harm** (or less harm than competitors) to consumers or the environment, including animals. This includes not harming anyone's physical or mental health.
- **Sell an honest product.** Don't claim that the product offers something it does not.
- **Use ethical supply chains.** If, for example, a clothing company claims to be ethical, they must be able to vouch for their supply chains (e.g. that no sweatshop or child labour is used; that inclusivity is practised when it comes to employees).
- **Be fair.** Is the product or service sold at a fair price? Are the policies fair for the consumer (e.g. return policies) and staff (e.g. fair pay)?
- **Be legal.** Has the company followed statutory or legal requirements? For example, licences are necessary for many products, including foods, toiletries and toys for children.

- **Include a corporate ethics code.** What is the company's position on their sense of responsibility to staff, consumers, supply chains, etc.?
- **Show respect.** All humans, from staff to suppliers and consumers, want to be treated with respect, especially during challenging times.
- **Show leadership.** Ethical leadership lies at the heart of all of the above. Good ethics needs to come from the person(s) who set up the business. It's unlikely a company with an unethical leader(s) will be able to follow ethical principles for long.
- **Be trustworthy.** This is integral. Consumers need to trust the product or service; staff need to be trusted to do their jobs; leaders need to trust their team and be trusted by staff to make positive decisions. Data protection is also a big issue. Businesses often have to collect personal data (email addresses, postal addresses, phone numbers), and these cannot be shared without the consumer's consent. The same rules apply to employee details.

From the ground up

Ethical values are built from the ground up and must always come from good leadership. I was recently talking to the CEO of Leeds Bradford Airport, who told me that he joined at a time when staff morale was very low due to all kinds of bad management decisions. He told me how, at 2 a.m. on a night shift, he spotted an escalator had just been repaired but needed cleaning; however, there was nobody nearby to help. Instead of calling someone, this CEO rolled up his sleeves and got stuck in.

At the sight of the boss scrubbing away on the airport floor, staff were shocked and impressed, and they really valued his humility. Immediately, his team felt boosted by watching him pitch in, and this spur-of-the-moment decision had a fantastic impact on staff morale.

The opposite of good leadership is letting the ego interfere, and this inevitably leads to issues within the company. Characteristics that should be avoided include being self-centred, being controlling, craving recognition, being competitive with other staff and being resistant to feedback.

The values I live by are these: work hard; have integrity; be honest and decent. 'Do as you would be done by' is an old saying, but it absolutely says it all. This is how I have run all my businesses.

We sat down and wrote a formal list of company values when BTL was getting started, and although my colleagues have changed the wording from time to time, the basic values are unchanged. They include working together with collaboration, flexibility, passion and creativity.

*

The reality is value systems for day-to-day work in a business must be informal. You have to live by values rather than write them down and expect them to work miraculously.

In all honesty, I wondered if our company values would still resonate and work on a practical level when our companies grew bigger in size. Surely our values would get diluted eventually? But they didn't.

This is because the employees who don't share our company values are the ones who don't tend to stay. Conversely, I have employed untrustworthy people (not that I knew at the time!) who, I later learned, ended up being positively affected by the honest culture.

We also value our employees' autonomy. I trust everyone to do their job (trust people until they don't prove trustworthy is another of my values), and I am happy for others to take credit for their work. In fact, I encourage staff to take credit, because they will care more about the product if they feel part of its development.

Reputation

Some years ago, there was an invitation for BTL to bid on an assessment contract and the client wanted the project finished within two years. We knew this was an impossible deadline, so suggested a more realistic time frame. Alas, we didn't get the contract. It went to a company that promised to deliver within 48 months, which, not surprisingly, they couldn't do in the end. They outsourced the project to India, and it went long overdue, then collapsed. I know of companies who even factor the fines they might receive for not delivering within the deadline into their overall costs at the start of a project.

Despite the loss of this contract, we chose the right path. Building a solid reputation that says your company is honest and realistic is a long-term strategy for success.

It takes a long time to build a good reputation and it can be destroyed in moments. Look at what happened to the Ratners

Group in the 1990s.[29] The owner, Gerald Ratner, made an offhand comment about the low quality of his jewellery at a conference, and this got picked up by newspaper reporters who put his comments on the front page. The value of his company plunged, and all his shops eventually shut down. If the founder of a company doesn't believe in their own product, how can they expect anyone else to?

Jim Collins, author of *Good to Great*, studied companies that continue to succeed over several generations of leaders and asked the central question: can a good company become a great company?

For Collins, for a leader to turn a good company into a great one, they need to be at the highest of five levels: 'Rather than relying on charisma or a big personality, a "level 5" leader builds enduring greatness through a paradoxical blend of personal humility and professional will. Without a level 5 leader at the helm, companies seldom achieve greatness.'

Transparency

In this online age, the veil can quickly be lifted on companies and their ethics, highlighting the importance of getting things right from the start. Very swiftly, a company's reputation can be made or broken by poor reviews or bad management. For example, if a customer makes a complaint online and the

---

[29] Daily Mail City & Finance Reporter, Gerald Ratner still reeling 30 years on from gaffe that sank his jewellery empire in a matter of seconds, *This Is Money* (23 April 2021), www.thisismoney.co.uk/money/markets/article-9505003/Gerald-Ratner-reeling-30-years-gaffe.html (accessed 19 March 2024).

response leads to an argument, it isn't going to look good. Addressing complaints should always be a priority and done in a thoughtful and calm manner. Offering to rectify the problem immediately or offer a refund is wise.

Conversely, if a customer has clearly had a good experience, then always ask for a review on Google, Amazon or wherever the product is available online.

Certification, based on tests and checks of the product, is another way of solidifying your company's ethical credentials. Certification may be awarded by government or accredited third parties. The standards and regulations vary depending on the country.

One type of certification is **B Corporation**, awarded to ethical businesses that work not just for profit, but to benefit people and the planet. 'Certified B Corporations, or B Corps, are companies verified by B Lab to meet high standards of social and environmental performance, transparency and accountability.'[30]

The B Corp certification was launched by B Lab, which was started in the US by three businessmen who wanted to make a difference. It has grown into a global vision. In the UK, there are over 1,900 businesses with B Corp status,[31] and it seems like a good target for any business to set.

---

[30] What does the B Corp certification mean? *B Lab Europe*, https://bcorporation.eu/what-is-a-b-corp/what-does-b-corp-certification-mean/#:~:text=Our%20non%2Dprofit%2C%20B%20Lab,to%20all%20of%20their%20stakeholders (accessed 25 March 2014).

[31] The UK B Corporation movement, *B Lab United Kingdom*, https://bcorporation.uk/# (accessed 10 March 2024).

The food industry is awash with certification of various kinds, and some have become synonymous with good quality – these include:

- **Fairtrade:** From tea to flowers to winter spice mix to fashion, there are over 6,000 fair trade products that promote global elimination of poverty and responsible consumerism.[32] Anything with the Fairtrade logo comes from farms that have been certified to provide fair wages and safe working conditions.
- **Soil Association:** They offer a logo that can be used on foods produced within an organic system. They have certified over 70% of organic food and drink bought in the UK.[33]
- **Rain Forest Alliance:** They provide certification for growers that meet a list of 'sustainable agriculture principles', including conserving local wildlife and water resources, treating workers fairly and reforesting.
- **Red Tractor:** They provide a logo for food and drink responsibly produced, packed, stored and transported

---

[32] Buying Fairtrade, *Fairtrade Foundation*, www.fairtrade.org.uk/buying-fairtrade/#:~:text=Buying%20Fairtrade%20is%20easy.,look%20for%20the%20FAIRTRADE%20Mark (accessed 10 March 2024).

[33] Food and drink organic certification, *Soil Association*, www.soilassociation.org/certification/food-drink/#:~:text=Today%2C%20Soil%20Association%20Certification%20still,the%20most%20recognised%20and%20trusted (accessed 10 March 2024).

in the UK. They take into consideration food safety, animal welfare and environmental protection.

- **Forest Stewardship Council (FSC):** They offer labelling for paper products that meet strict standards for woodland care and certification for companies that are committed to sustainable use of forest materials.

There is a growing number of certifications to reflect the climate issue too, with low carbon, net zero or offsetting schemes. No certification is bullet-proof, however. Criticism has been levelled at Red Tractor for not doing regular checks on farms, and at the Rain Forest Alliance for only requiring 30% of a product's ingredients to match their standards before the label can be used.

The website www.ethicalconsumer.org provides details on the policies and actions of 40,000 plus brands.

Case study: tales from a mountain top

Outdoor clothing companies have shown ground-breaking ethical leadership when it comes to factoring in people and the environment as part of their operations. One example often cited, for good reason, is the outdoor clothing brand Patagonia...

Back in the 1970s, founder Yvon Chouinard was a climber who taught himself blacksmithing and invented new pitons, a reusable hardware that climbers bang into the rocks to use as an anchor for their climb. He started selling them for $1.50 and grew a small business. They became bestsellers. By 1970, Chouinard was the leading supplier in the US. However, environmentalists began to criticize the product because climbers repeatedly hammered them into popular climbing routes, damaging the rocks.

Despite the product making up 70% of Chouinard's business, the decision was made to phase pitons out and instead develop aluminium chockstones, which can be wedged in by hand rather than needing to be hammered in. The risk was worthwhile, as the new product took off quickly.

But Chouinard didn't stop there. Three years later, he founded Patagonia, a climbing clothing company that started by importing rugby shirts from the UK and reselling to climbers. They went on to introduce groundbreaking practices, including a commitment to using organic cotton only and making the first fleece using 100% recycled bottles. Since 1985, the company has been using 1% of all profits to support grassroots environmental companies all over the world. The company has set up support for employees too, offering an on-site vegetarian cafe and childcare.

In 2022, Chouinard and his family decided to ensure all company profits go towards the fight against climate change and the protection of undeveloped lands. They have done this by transferring ownership of Patagonia to the Patagonia Purpose Trust and the not-for-profit organization Holdfast Collective. The amount of money generated is expected to be around $100 million (£78 million) in the second year.[34]

'Building the best product while causing the least harm is at the heart of what we do,' says Yvon Chouinard.[35]

What stands out with Chouinard's company is that he ditched a product that wasn't good for the environment and invented something else. He innovated after listening to his customer base, even though in the short term it must have affected profits. This long-term thinking led to long-term success.

The feel-good factor of giving

Forging charitable links with local communities is good for ethical networking and boosts the positive image of any start-up, not to mention the bonus of boosting staff morale. We all feel better about ourselves when we do something for someone else, especially if they are in less fortunate

---

[34] David Gelles, Billionaire no more: founder gives away the company, *The New York Times* (14 September 2022), www.nytimes.com/2022/09/14/climate/patagonia-climate-philanthropy-chouinard.html (accessed 19 March 2024).

[35] Patagonia shows how turning a profit doesn't have to cost the Earth, *McKinsey & Company* (20 April 2023), www.mckinsey.com/industries/agriculture/our-insights/patagonia-shows-how-turning-a-profit-doesnt-have-to-cost-the-earth# (accessed 12 March 2024).

circumstances. Showing kindness to others boosts self-esteem and reaps worthwhile wealth.

Emma Gilmartin, who heads Surpass Assessment's charity committee, explains that

> The overall vision of Surpass is to improve education, so we have specifically chosen charities to reflect this, especially focusing on charities to help children.

> We donate to food and clothing banks, to help children get fed and clothed. We also set up a volunteer scheme for our staff to visit a local primary school to hear children read. We do small things too, like bake sales and potluck lunches to raise more money for a local mental health charity. This provides a communal activity for staff and gives everyone a boost and a chance to mingle.

> Few people are able to give time to charities, so donating money is another tangible way to make a difference to contribute.

> We make everything count, and whether it's time or money, it provides a boost to both the charities and staff alike.

Nev Percy is one of the employees who took time out to volunteer. He listened to local primary school children reading their books, to help them develop basic reading skills and comprehension.

> We listened to each child for 15 minutes a week, and it's hard to put into words what benefits it bought to us all. The schools were always very effusive with

their thanks and the children couldn't wait to join in, with many excitedly lining up to have a turn. Afterwards, I always walked away with a spring in my step and a glow that would last all day. Everyone speaks well of the experience, both the children and those listening to them.

At one point, a friend of mine came to me to ask for help. His grandson had dropped out of college and spent his days video gaming and little else. He asked if I could help him find a job. So we put this young man into the Surpass technology department and gave him training to see how he got on.

Over time, this young man ended up gaining tech skills that put him on a career path, and he made a huge success out of. It was a pleasure to help turn his life around.

Aside from helping individuals, where possible, there are so many ways to support the local community, including: buying products or resources from local charities; donating a percentage of profits; sponsoring a particular project; donating time (e.g. becoming a brand ambassador or offering specialist skills or knowledge); and offering work experience to vulnerable people.

Giving of yourself to others is a cornerstone of worthwhile wealth.

Further reading

Sarah Duncan, *The Ethical Business Book: A Practical, Non-Preachy Guide to Business Sustainability* (2021).

Julia Davenport, *The Green Start Up: Make Your Business Better for the Planet* (2022).

9

Embracing risk

In this chapter, I examine:

- The importance of resilience
- The need for mentors
- How to reframe a 'risk' as an 'experiment'
- The need for patience

It is better to light a candle than to curse the darkness.

—Chinese proverb

'You're talking about my husband,' says a Canadian doctor who I am chatting to while climbing in Glencoe, Scotland. 'He absolutely hates his job.'

While navigating a steep rocky slope and peering over a vast ledge, we were discussing why people stay in jobs they don't like. This lady loves her work as a consultant but feels terribly sad for her husband, who is a mortgage advisor. In an ideal world, he'd pursue a more creative enterprise, but he is clinging to security instead.

Her comments, as we clamber over the rocky terrain, make me consider the risks involved in not taking a risk. Right now, I could easily turn an ankle, but this breathtaking vantage point feels so good for my soul that the risk feels worthwhile. Plus, I'm looking where I put my feet to minimize the chance of toppling over.

In this moment, my favourite quote pops up again: *'Nothing is worth doing without one leg over the precipice.'*

We must take risks to grow as people, grow in character, grow in courage and ultimately grow in business if that's what we're trying to do. Without risk of any kind, growth of any kind is impossible. Every single day, we encounter risks but often think nothing of it. However, when it comes to a start-up, the risk feels too overwhelming for many.

Like the Canadian doctor's husband, dreaming and not doing leads to a lifetime of regret and missed opportunities to grow worthwhile wealth. Arguably, missing out on a life of enrichment is the biggest risk of all.

Believe in your own resilience

The majority of people have no idea how resilient they are until they try something new or find themselves tackling an extreme situation. Like kids wanting ice cream, we have all got an innate persistence that drives us to overcome any challenge if we choose to lean into it. The human psyche grows once we overcome a perceived risk.

In my life, the best things I have achieved have involved stepping outside my comfort zone – a place many of us become trapped in, because it feels safe there. But this becomes a 'tramline' state of existence, where we operate on autopilot.

What would your ambition be if you could do *anything*? If one message comes out of this book loud and clear, I want it to be: **the risk is worth the reward**.

In the face of risks, any entrepreneur can work on developing the strengths they'll need. A supportive network is one huge element. When we feel supported or have observed someone else successfully doing what we want to do, it immediately ignites a feeling of inward courage and optimism.

Asking for help or guidance can feel challenging, but the fact is, most potential mentors love to be asked. They are flattered and want to help others, as this promotes the feel-good factor.

Mentors

One of the most effective ways of gaining lasting resilience is to find a mentor for regular feedback and operational advice. This doesn't have to be in an official capacity – there are people around us who, through casual friendships, can inspire us to do better or achieve our goals.

Observing someone else doing what you want to do first fast-tracks confidence and promotes action.

My father was my first mentor. Despite working very hard for a family business, which I felt at times he didn't enjoy, he remained upbeat and positive, and exuded a wonderful energy. He enjoyed a flourishing social life with a wide circle of friends from all backgrounds. By living simply and enjoying his time off, he revealed to me that worthwhile wealth came from a life outside of the grind of work.

Another man I came across early in life through HF Holidays taught me a huge amount about business leadership and doing things your own way with good values at heart.

Peter Brassey was appointed Chief Executive of HF Holidays when he was 36. At the same time, I became Chair at 33. We were both exceptionally young for these roles, but I couldn't help noticing how Peter operated. He 'walked the walk' instead of simply talking.

In his first morning on the job, he took a sledgehammer and broke down the reserved signs for senior managers in the car park. Well, he tried to – he couldn't break them, so he got a handyman to finish the job. Back then, in the 1980s, many managers were very autocratic, so this act of defiance to make parking a level playing field was quite groundbreaking.

Peter kept breaking the mould, and I was impressed by all he did. He was very good at replacing people when they did not fit in and he let them go with kindness, in such a way that they understood and accepted it. He had a good understanding of the culture of the business and was always meeting the clients, listening carefully to what they had to say. Indeed, he even went on the HF Holidays with his wife and threw himself into them – the only way to understand the holiday experience.

He was very intuitive too. For example, he went ahead with the idea of unlimited self-selection for customer packed lunches when his colleagues advised that it would be prohibitively costly.

He was proved right, partly because people responded honestly and partly because food costs were a relatively small proportion of total costs. I also learned from him about hiring valuable talent even when not sure exactly what slot there would be for the person concerned. Finally, he was also a very good strategic thinker and put the company on a very sound financial footing that lasted for many years.

Tragically, Peter died in 1992 in an unlucky accident while walking in the Pyrenees. He was never formally a mentor, but in reality, I learned more from Peter than anyone else.

Bob's musings from a mountain top

We all face challenges and need to get through them. The ways I have stayed resilient at different times include:

- **Keeping a sense of perspective.** Business is not a matter of life and death and indeed it is not as important as family and friends. People will be remarkably supportive if you share your worries, however, so be honest about what's happening if you need help.
- **Protecting the 'downside'.** Think about what could go wrong, and as far as possible ensure that it will not be too disastrous. Do not, for example, put your home or life savings on the line.
- **Hanging on to a bill-paying job as long as possible**, so that the business can fully afford you when you do join full time. This is particularly useful in the case of a new product or service, as you may not know how long it will take for the idea to take off.
- **Relying on a partner or your own savings.** If you can rely on someone who is in a secure, well-paid job or if you're lucky enough to have some spare cash,

use that. But if you don't have anything like this, then start in a market that you know will work quickly or prove the point by getting some real sales before investing too much.

- Having an upbeat saying to tell yourself when things go wrong. My favourites are:
  - If it was easy everybody would be doing it.
  - Nothing worthwhile was ever achieved without one leg over the precipice.
  - The consequences of the risk I am taking here is nothing compared with the risks I took when, as a young man, I enjoyed rock climbing.
- Finally, my wife's advice: **exercise, eat well** (i.e. don't overdo meals with ingredients your grandmother would not recognize) and be careful to **limit alcohol consumption**. I do a short run every morning, walk whenever I can, cycle and swim. Just in case I sound a bit too virtuous, I also like a pint.

Case study: tales from a mountain top

Deciding to take a risk often comes from a place of passion. Trusting gut instinct is what Bridget van Oosterhout did when she had a career change in her mid-forties, giving up everything she knew for the worthwhile wealth she found in the great outdoors…

In the early 2000s, I went away on holiday with HF Holidays to walk around Glencoe in the Scottish Highlands for the first time.

The moment I arrived, I felt hit by lightning, because it felt like a homecoming. When I returned to the Netherlands, I immediately booked a return trip. Then every year for seven years I went back to Scotland, always feeling inexplicably 'at home' there. Although very happy in my managerial job for the Steiner organization, I wondered if it would ever be possible to go and live in the Scottish Highlands. I even started watching golf championships on TV when they were held in Scotland; it got silly really!

Every year I visited the same hotel called Alltshellach, near Ballachulish, and the manager got to know me quite well.

Then, unexpectedly, I was made redundant from my job and felt quite devastated, as my work had always been such an important factor in my life. On my usual summer Scottish holiday, I got chatting to the manager, who told me they were short-staffed. I had no experience at all of working in hospitality, but not wanting to return home, I offered my services.

I moved all my things into a staff room that was like a nun's cell, and I used a shared bathroom for 11 people. Usually, I wouldn't accept such hardship at my stage of life, but to be able to remain in the Highlands made the risk feel worthwhile.

After a fortnight, the manager offered me a job for the rest of the season, including wintertime. I wasn't sure how I would cope with a Scottish winter, but I went home, rented out my flat and returned to Scotland.

People back home thought I was mad, giving up a whole life because I loved the scenery of a place, but the peace and joy the Glencoe region brought me made everything worthwhile.

Usually, I am not good at making decisions, but this felt easy to make even if I was risking everything by giving up all I had known. I completed the winter season happily and was then offered a position in hotel management full time.

This was a job I'd never previously considered doing, but grew to love. Welcoming other tourists to a place I loved came naturally.

At the end of the season, someone asked me if I was 'going home' to the Netherlands, and I replied: 'This is my home now and always has been.'

It took me six years to buy a place of my own, big enough for all my belongings, but the wait was worth it.

Twenty years later, I am planning on retiring here. It has been an incredible experience. Hard work at times but living in such a heavenly place has made everything worthwhile. I always think a person should follow their gut, follow their heart. You can never live with regrets then.

Reframe the 'risk' as an 'experiment'

A scientific background has helped me enormously when it comes to taking risks in both life and business. The word 'risk' is unhelpful. None of us like the idea of risking things, especially when it comes to precious time and finances.

Instead of considering our business or life decisions as 'risks', consider them 'experiments'.

All scientists take risks to conduct experiments. A scientist chooses a theory and an untested hypothesis, then sets up a series of experiments involving a methodical process to prove or disprove the hypothesis.

This will inevitably involve failures, so they should be expected. This mindset is what all scientists accept at the beginning of any experiment. They will go from failure to failure, observing and tweaking until they have the optimum conditions and manage to find a conclusion to their findings.

The point is that the 'failure' is not considered a negative; rather, it is simply part of an ongoing process of experimentation. The word 'failure' is not even used in fact, because there is no right or wrong in an experiment – there is simply a learning event.

It is important to be ruthlessly objective, however. Was the prediction or hypothesis wrong?

It is very tempting to come up with 'explanations' after the event. Some people do it all the time. How often have I heard people blaming low holiday bookings at HF Holidays on an early Easter or a late Easter, yet somehow the Easter effect was never predicted and mitigated in advance.

The most important thing is to compare your predictions with the outcomes and learn from the result. It is true in science, and it is true in business. It is probably true in other walks of life too, but 'confirmation bias' often leads to people failing to learn.

Scientists are (or should be) pragmatic and realistic right from the start. They do not expect immediate success and keep an open mind. They are generally patient and follow the steps, not judging what the outcome will be. Of course, often scientists do think they know what the outcome will be, or at least hope for a particular outcome, but they have to accept and try to understand if they are wrong. It is much the same in business. For example, we make predictions about our sales, and if they turn out to be too high (or indeed too low), then we need to try to understand why we did not get it right so that we can do better next time. In brief, just as scientists try to get a better understanding of some aspect of nature, so in business we try to get a better understanding of the behaviour of the market.

Scientists must also try and be creative, within the constraints of their specialism. Finding creativity in a straitjacket is a skill any entrepreneur must foster, because there will always be all kinds of constraints in business (finance, time, expertise, market constraints).

Einstein was exceptionally good at judging what pathways to pursue then breaking down his theoretical work into a series of tiny steps. Indeed, he once commented that physics consisted of a series of simple steps. People who find learning physics hard have usually missed out a step – this is what I used to say to students. The same is true with business skills.

If you can't see a way through a challenge, break the situation down and go back a step, seeking advice from those who have gone before.

Patience

> Adopt the pace of Nature. Her secret is patience.
> —Ralph Waldo Emerson[36]

In her book *The Long Win*, Cath Bishop talks about winning as not being a fixed moment in time. Neither is succeeding in business. Whether running a famous high street store like Marks & Spencer or a new start-up, there will be peaks and troughs, ups and downs. Expect these statistical fluctuations, with things going well and badly, but know you can keep going.

It's easy to get distracted with an emotional state of mind, so be wary of getting caught up with unrealistic expectations when passionate about a particular idea or in a panic about finances, etc. This is what happens to venture capitalists who want the big bucks without practising the patience or strategy behind it.

Nobody shares the full details of their cost and profits, so new entrepreneurs get shocked at how precarious the nature of business is. It's the long, slow win, the one where we pace ourselves, like on any decent walk.

---

[36] R.W. Emerson, Education, *The Complete Writings of Ralph Waldo Emerson* (1929).

Finding support

Finding a business mentor has never been easier with the internet and communities that have formed online. For example, mentorsme (www.mentorsme.co.uk) offers business owners to find a mentor online, and Be the Business (www.bethebusiness.com) is a not-for-profit organization set up to help business start-ups.

Also look at local Facebook groups, local business networking groups and LinkedIn to find potential mentors in your industry.

10

Mitigating risks

In this chapter, I examine:
- The most common risks every new business faces
- How to mitigate these risks
- What should be included in a business plan or mitigation plan

The risk of a new business failing is well documented. The rate of failure for a start-up in the UK is 60% within the first three years and 20% in the first year.[37] This is sobering, and for most people, the idea of taking such a risk in the face of such poor chances of success means they will never try.

But it is my belief that ALL risks can be mitigated against. There is a myriad of common and preventable reasons for business failure, and this means risks can be identified, understood and minimized.

The biggest and most common risks to any new start-up include cash flow problems, not understanding the market

[37] Joe Hinton, The top six reasons small businesses fail – and how you can avoid them! *UNBM* (27 June 2023), www.ukbusinessmentoring.co.uk/news/why-do-businesses-fail (accessed 19 March 2024).

properly, bad supply chains, being rejected and overreliance on grants.

Here, I examine each of these risks in turn.

Running out of money

Poor cashflow is the biggest cause of UK business failures. A recent study revealed that 82% of new businesses fail due to poor cash flow or lack of understanding of cash flow.[38] The next biggest risk (79%) is lack of initial investment – trying to set up a business with too little money.

The golden rule is simple: if what goes out (expenses) is less than what is coming in, then there will be a cash flow problem.

But how can you foresee cash flow issues? There are many ways, and some are easy to overlook.

First off, 'if you don't have the brass, don't spend it' is a wise Yorkshire saying that I live by. Reducing unnecessary expenditure is key, so make sure you're tracking what is coming in and manage inventory properly. Do not commit to overheads before the business is ready. This is tempting to do, but really keep all costs to an absolute minimum.

This is the time to rope in family, friends or anyone you know with relevant experience who can offer their services for free.

---

[38] Jerry Vance, Small business cash flow management: strategies for success, *Preferred CFO* (29 November 2023), https://preferredcfo. com/cash-flow-reason-small-businesses-fail (accessed 19 March 2024).

In the early days, I offered a friend shares in a business in exchange for his time, as I had little cash. He's done very well out of this now!

Don't be afraid to ask for help in whatever form. People are often open to helping, especially if they believe in the new product or service. When my brother began designing and doing the tech work for my CD-ROMs, I offered him royalties of 10%, an income which steadily grew.

The gross margins in your business are the difference between the sale price and the cost of delivering that sale. In practice, the rate at which a business can grow without running out of cash (known as overtrading) depends on the size of the gross margins. The tighter the gross margins, the bigger the danger of overtrading. In general, business-to-business sales tend to have bigger margins and bigger sales than business-to-consumer sales. Again, brace yourself for the fluctuations. This is necessary because the human brain is wired to believe things will stay the same. For example, if your product is flying out the door, you will be delighted and believe sales will continue like this. Same for if no stock is shifting – it's easy to get psychologically worn down and struggle to imagine sales ever picking up.

If your business is market led, a business plan can help mitigate the costs. But if it's ideas or tech led, it's possible to survive far into the future until the company takes off, usually by staying on in your existing job. Whatever way you manage to find the finance, never put your house on the line.

It's best to be overly pessimistic about cash flow in the first few years. So, even if the forecast is good, factor in the challenges, such as suppliers or sales slowing, or a supplier letting you down. Often those are the pinch areas.

Try and spot the early warning signs of poor cash flow – for example, you could research customers or suppliers to make sure they have good reviews or ratings where possible. Make sure you implement standard terms and conditions in any payment contracts so that you can chase prompt payments and include penalties for late payments. Always create a cash flow forecast, and monitor it very regularly so you can see exactly what is coming in and out each week. Hard months can include those with holidays, such as over Christmas or in summer, so factor those in.

Also, most entrepreneurs won't be able to afford to pay a regular wage to themselves for quite a while. This comes as a shock to some people, but any profits are likely to need to go back into the business at first. Accepting this is necessary in the early days.

Not understanding the market

You could have the greatest ideas in the world, but if people don't want your service or product, then it's not going to work. If the market you wish to enter is reasonably well understood, then this is where the quality and quantity of market research comes in. Poor research is another common cause of failure.

Look at your competitors – what are they doing well and badly? Where can your product fit in? A proven market is a good litmus test, as it's a sign there's a market for your product, but will yours offer something better? Different?

Why will a customer choose your product over something else? If you can, ask them!

Do you know where potential buyers can be found? Are you able to stock your item there?

This does not work however when you are creating a brand-new product or idea. Sometimes an idea can be so original that no one can visualize what it would be like, and so market research can be rather meaningless. The first iPhone is a good example of this, but there are many other examples in the field of technology.

In 2014, we organized our first international conference for Surpass customers and employees, bringing people together to share ideas. That led us to offer new ideas directly to the customer base and proved vital to developing and testing new product theories. Especially when we asked people if they'd chip in. Whether people put money towards developing an idea quickly reveals how much a new product or service is wanted or needed.

Find your customer base and ask them what they want, if you can. This is preferably done face to face in casual conversation in their natural environment, or it can be in a more formal setting or via a survey if need be. It's priceless information.

Bad suppliers

This is a big challenge, because until you have worked with suppliers, it's hard to know how reliable they will be. This is where word of mouth or networking can increase the likelihood of successfully finding good eggs. Research companies' reputations, either online or through colleagues. Make sure they are reliable and ethical. You can't promote an ethical product if the source supplier doesn't share your values. Follow the supply chain as far as it goes as well.

This is an area in which you can gain a lot by talking to other businesses about the suppliers they use. In the past, I have wasted a huge amount of time dealing with bad suppliers, and I think that some of the best help stemmed from others guiding me to people who provide a good product or a reliable service.

Rejection

Having the door slam shut when you approach people you need assistance or permission from is very common. This is especially true of middle managers and those working in local authorities.

The quote 'Strong advocates have little to gain if all goes well and a lot to lose if it goes wrong' is attributed to Gerald M. Weinberg, an influential computer scientist, author and consultant. It reflects the idea that individuals who passionately advocate for a particular outcome or solution may have less to gain if things go as planned, since their stance is already in alignment with the expected outcome so they have no more work to do. However, if things don't go as anticipated, they could face significant consequences or loss of credibility due to their strong advocacy.

That said, an entrepreneur looking to do something differently has everything to gain if a permission is needed, so keep plugging away. Just be clear, concise, and prepared for questioning and a cynical response.

If possible, avoid layers of bureaucracy and identify the person at the top to ask permission. Go straight to them, as they will have the flexibility and freedom to have strategic thoughts, hopefully granting permission for what is needed.

Overreliance on grants

There are many start-up loans and grants available for new businesses. A whole raft will pop up in an online search, but be wary of what you're signing up for. Many grants come with strings attached, leading to jumping through hoops and taking the business founder away from their original vision or the 'why' of the business.

Some start-ups sadly end up having to spend half their time chasing new investment grants to keep going, diverting the precious time and energy of those involved away from the actual business they love.

There are many groups, such as AD:VENTURE, based in Leeds, which offer development support and guidance, and can signpost where suitable grants might be available. The LEP Network (www.lepnetwork.net), which recently lost their government funding, have local hubs that support small businesses – especially important in the current economic crisis.

It is worth bearing in mind that there is no repeat business in grants – they are one-off source of funding. If I make a sale to a customer, I can hope that many sales will follow, provided my product or service is good. A grant does not carry that benefit. In addition, winning a grant doesn't provide any learning about the market. My companies have accessed grants when they were small, and that helped at times, but in general, I have always been happier when all my income comes from sales to willing buyers.

*

In business-speak, other risks include:

- **Compliance risks:** These risks occur when your company doesn't comply with industry standards, and each industry has different standards. I faced this hurdle with my audiometer. Back then, I was able to certify what was needed myself, but things have changed now and costs would be involved. Check what your business needs to comply with.
- **Reputational risks:** This is when a strategy fails and the start-up faces the court of public opinion or loss of overall industry reputation, causing a fall in early profits. These risks occur when mistakes are made due to poor planning or strategy. This is where setting out good ethical practice can help.
- **Legal risks:** This is when government rules for companies get broken or indeed the law is broken. Insider knowledge on the legal part of your industry is a must-have. Seek professional advice on this whenever in doubt.
- **Operational risks:** This is where the day-to-day running of the business ends up draining the profits – for example, running into unnecessary costs that are not foreseen, and which add up, is a common risk.

More personal risk factors that could thwart new start-ups include:

- **Running out of energy.** My advice, echoing my wife's, is to eat well and exercise! It's obvious but it's worth taking the time out to rebalance. Founding a business can be very time-consuming and involve much plate spinning. Of course, once it's up and running, we can aim to make the business work around our lives, but at least in the beginning, long hours may be needed.

- **Loneliness.** Join local business networks, either on Facebook or through business forums, or find like-minded entrepreneurs online. This would have made my early days far easier. Always be open to meeting new people and gleaning new ideas from conversations.

- **Following the wrong advice.** The trouble is you won't know until you have done this. That's why finding a decent mentor early on to ask and double-check others' advice is a good idea. Accept things WILL go wrong despite best intentions, but spotting this as soon as possible and changing paths is what mitigates the risks.

- **Loss of support system (e.g. spouse, family).** If your partner or other family members have helped financially or emotionally to support the new project and withdraw this support, it's a big knock. Put a backup in place from the start.

- **Losing faith or enthusiasm for the idea.** This is very common at times. It's almost impossible to keep up relentless Labrador-like energy, unless you're one of those talented salespeople who can keep the enthusiasm high at all times. Expect peaks and troughs, and if you believe in the WHY of the business and your overarching motivations, it makes it easier to stick things out.

- **Unrealistic expectations leading to any of the above.** It is really common to start a project filled with extreme enthusiasm, all cylinders firing, and then after several major blows feel utterly defeated. Be realistic and expect knockbacks. Any business, regardless of size or success, is full of them. If you expect them, then you're more likely to think objectively about a way out of them.

Mitigating risks

Only those who will risk going too far can possibly find out just how far one can go.

—T.S. Eliot

Risk comes from not knowing what you're doing.

—Warren Buffet

The quotes above are examples of two extremes. Don't risk going too far too fast and don't take the leap into the void before preparing a descent. Rather, try to understand what you're doing at each step, to avoid disaster. This isn't easy.

Learning how to minimize risks is one of the hardest things a new businessperson faces. The situation is often compared to that of a duck on water. From the outside, all our staff or customers can see is us gliding along, but underneath the feet are waggling like crazy.

You must keep on top of the details to make it a success. I truly believe the start-ups that sadly fail are the ones that didn't gain these understandings before starting out.

Case study: tales from a mountain top

Dr Amjad Pervez took a huge risk giving up a lucrative career in finance to run a corner shop. But what appeared to be a mad decision led to building one of the UK's biggest specialist cash and carries and a business empire…

I had a career working in financial services for a building society when my father approached me to ask if I would help set up a family business. He was a war veteran and wanted to invest his pension into buying a local corner shop.

This felt like a huge risk, but I'd already discovered the corporate world was not for me. I didn't like the hierarchal structure, which bred a culture of lethargic performance. In order to get anything done, permission was needed from so many unnecessary gatekeepers, including the board, and this was frustrating.

With a young family and children, it felt like a big risk to give up the security, however I knew I wanted to do something different with my future.

For this venture to succeed, I made an agreement with Dad that I would be the one to make the business decisions and he had to allow me to do this. I had seen other families in business becoming marred by family politics and wanted to avoid this. We trusted each other this was how it would work, and thankfully it did. I had to make this work; there was no plan B.

We took over a corner shop in Bradford which was in a terrible state. As we made repairs, I started my research to see what customers in the local area were looking for, and it was Afro-Caribbean food, fresh, quality fruit and vegetables, toiletries and frozen foods. The nearest stockists of Afro-Caribbean products were in Leeds and Huddersfield, an hour away on a bus. So we started off stocking these products, marketing these heavily in the local area.

I continued to look closely at the trends. This was during the Thatcher years, when more women were going back to work part time and the sales of frozen ready meals were rising, so we pivoted towards these. They provided a good margin and customers would often shop with us three times a week.

When it comes to mitigating risk, the most important consideration is to choose the product–market fit. Whatever product you're trying to sell, ask yourself: 'Does it relieve any existing pain for the customer?' Quality and service became the backbone of our family business as we tried to give customers what they wanted.

I also looked at my local community and realized we were near a hospital, so we stocked items like flowers, cards and small gifts. I would give flowers to loyal customers for free, so they would feel appreciated. We set up a loyalty reward scheme too, for repeat business. This generosity came from a genuine place and our customers realized this.

Five years into the business, we bought the post office next door and expanded into the video hire sector, but meanwhile the social trends in food needs continued developing.

With more people going abroad on package holidays, we had customers wanting to eat international foods back home, so we started to supply Mediterranean and Asian cuisine ingredients and ready meals.

I also built a supportive network outside of my community. This meant I wasn't just speaking to Asian businesspeople but English, Chinese and Jewish people to see what their advice would be. One local businessman, Barry Fuller, from Fuller International foods in Leeds, became an important mentor. He advised me never to compete with the supermarkets nearby, but offer something different. I am grateful to have listened to this advice, because it worked.

Meanwhile, restaurant owners asked if we could sell food items in bulk, things like oil, yoghurt, rice, flour and seafood. I spotted that the margins on seafood were very good, so we found global suppliers to create a robust supply chain solution.

I realized seafood was needed in every kind of cuisine, from Italian to Chinese, to pizza and fish and chip shops, so that's when Seafresh took off and we moved into the wholesale frozen food sector.

We continued to ask our customers what they needed, and many suggested home deliveries. The uptick in sales went crazy, which caused lot of business management problems. In order to solve these issues, we used the services of Business Link, a government support organization, which suggested practical ways of implementing solutions. This process was lengthy and took almost six months to complete. However, the improved management systems meant we could now scale without much pain.

One of the biggest mitigations against the risk of a business failing is to get continual feedback from the customers. Don't ask once; ask all the time. You need the information – the good, the bad and the ugly – in order to know the true situation. With the right information, one is able to innovate and change accordingly. This helps cement the loyalty of customers and builds a community of loyal customers who go out and become your ambassadors for new customer referrals, which every business needs.

Our value proposition or uniqueness was that we were probably the first cash and carry group which offered the widest range of food ingredients for all catering sectors, all under one roof and delivered to the doorstep at extremely competitive prices. Our tag line became: 'One call delivers all.'

Slowly but surely with the right team (which is utterly customer-centric), our business has grown steadily, and now we have eight outlets, called Adams Food Services, in major cities, selling thousands of products, including cleaning and packaging equipment. With the emergence of e-commerce, we have quickly adopted the new technologies to ensure that our customers can easily shop the way they feel comfortable. We also provide click and collect, click and deliver, or ordering through our popular company app.

Our business is now structured as a holding group and is one the largest specialist cash and carry group networks in the UK, a dream that began from a corner shop.

Business plan

The entrance strategy is actually more important than the exit strategy.

–Edward Lampert, Sears Holdings

For a market-led start-up, where it's necessary to raise finance and attract investors, you will need a business plan.

This plan will evolve, and you must be able to change it as you go; however, a standard plan should include:

- An executive summary description of the company
- An analysis of the products or services
- A marketing and sales strategy
- A description of how management will operate
- Financial projections
- The funding request (side note: in the UK, we have an aversion to talking about money – many plans can be vague and woolly on this all-important subject, but you should spell out exactly what you're asking for)
- An appendix with supporting documents (this includes information about the team behind the venture, market research, legal documents and images relating to products or services)

When it comes to five-year projections, often they are a waste of time. It's great to have big aspirations, but spending time and energy focusing on where you see the summit of your business being is often pointless at an early stage. No business plan ever has an unhappy ending! Instead, focusing on the cash flow, investments if needed and then expansion if necessary is a better use of limited time and resources.

When people approach me for investment, I look for talented people who share my interests. Those who come well prepared, understand our company's background and want to engage openly about exactly what their requirements are always look like a very good prospect.

A mitigation plan as well as a business plan

For tech-led or ideas-led start-ups, a mitigation plan is another good idea. This kind of plan is arguably more important than a business plan for tech start-ups, as sudden changes in technology can lead to a radical change of plan. The mitigation plan is not there to eliminate risk, as this is impossible, but to take actionable decisions when they arise.

The aim is to make risks tolerable for your business to survive and flourish. So how does a new start-up plan for these risks? First, make it a priority. Write a list of all the identifiable risks and start collecting this data. What are the riskiest parts of the business? If you don't like the look of the sales figures or see a bottleneck or pinch point, delve deeper to find out why. Is it because of the time of year? Has the market changed? Have the suppliers changed?

Monitor what is different and what stays the same. In a new start-up, it's easy to get distracted by other problems or other potential shiny things over there that can provide much-needed distraction. Don't get sucked into thinking issues will go away of their own accord. They never do. Confront the challenges methodically and head-on. There is nobody who can do this but you.

Strategies to mitigate general risks

There are various proven strategies to mitigate risk:

- **Acceptance.** Decide what risks are inevitable for your kind of business. Taking advice from those who have a similar business could be a good idea here. Knowing what you must accept helps identify what you cannot control and, therefore, what you can control.

- **Transference.** What third party can take the risk for you? For example, insurance companies can insure against many risks. Or can you write commitments for suppliers into contracts?

- **Minimize the risks.** Where can this be factored in? For example, if your costs are skyrocketing due to a price increase in raw materials, could you find them cheaper elsewhere or tweak the composition of the product without reducing quality? Or if you're losing time doing too much yourself within the business, can you outsource any of those jobs?

- **Avoidance.** This is the biggest risk and can kill the business. So if, for example, you loathe bookkeeping, definitely outsource this, as we all need to sort paperwork to pay our taxes. Or if you need extra pairs of hands to complete a project because you risk not reaching the market on time, then find out what help is affordable to get things done.

- **Cash flow.** As mentioned, this is often the most fatal risk, so address it before anything else. Increasing sales is often the solution, how can this be done?

Years ago, my dad used to say: 'Don't try and cross your bridges until you come to them.' Basically, you can't pre-empt every single little risk. Many problems might not even happen (remember False Evidence Appearing Real), and often it's only in the doing (once you are on the bridge) that you can learn to react to the unexpected ones.

If you have made a mitigation plan and have educated yourself about common start-up risks, then you've done the best by your new business and are giving it the best chance of success.

Further reading

Michael Buckworth, *Built on Rock: The Busy Entrepreneur's Legal Guide to Start-up Success* (2021).

11

The importance of innovation

In this chapter, I examine:

- The importance of a growth mindset
- The lean start-up model
- Planting and timing of ideas

> You can't solve a problem on the same level that it was created. You have to rise above it to the next level.
>
> —Albert Einstein

Your business idea is likely to involve one exciting idea. You have probably thought about this non-stop for months, years even. You may have told family and friends (who are hopefully supportive!) and may have imagined your product on shop shelves or your service being used, or having a brand name that makes everyone smile.

But hang on a minute. As much as I want to encourage these dreams of success, the need to innovate must remain on the table, even in the very early days. Even when you think you've got your business model and market sussed.

Why?

Because all new entrepreneurs, whatever the type or size of business, need to keep their minds open to flexibility and change right from the start. This is because business and markets change constantly and often when we least expect. One of the biggest risks to mitigate is a change in market conditions.

*

There will always be better and easier or more productive ways of operating your business. There will always be tweaks or pivots or unforeseen challenges in the market. Technology or social media trends and markets change all the time. It's important to keep pace with all developments.

Whatever your start-up is, innovation is about adapting to give your business the best chance of success. To make a business that flourishes, you also need to keep your vision of worthwhile wealth in mind. If your business no longer serves your lifestyle, then change is necessary again.

Like a walk, we always set off with expectations of good weather, good conversations, a straightforward journey and a glow of accomplishment once we reach the summit. But no journey is smooth. Rain can cloud the vision. You could reach the summit with a headache, or the view could be spoiled by a loud group of ramblers, or the heavens could open and you didn't bring your waterproofs...

In retrospect, the part of the walk you end up enjoying the most could be a cracking conversation or the discovery of an unexpected waterfall on the way. The actual journey could be something to remember rather than the destination.

We manage our expectations of business like we manage our expectations of walks. There is no straightforward path to follow without bumps along the way. The trajectory might always look smooth for others but never yourself, as in life. A founder is never able to sit back and think '*I've reached the summit at last*' either, because a new challenge will always be around the corner. That's not to say you can't enjoy the views and successes on the way.

It's all in the mind

When our customers ask us why we can't do this or try that, we can experiment to see if we can. I call these **incremental innovations**. These are small tweaks we can do to change something. For example, our product Surpass is used for on-screen exams, and clients often ask for new question types to be available. Creating a new question type is an incremental innovation.

The big picture ideas (and for a start-up it's likely to be a big picture idea) lead to **radical innovations**.

Once you get going, it is important to think about radical innovations as well as the incremental possibilities, although in practice this may not be easy until you are some way down the line. However, having a few radical innovations in your back pocket is great protection against your main line of business going wrong for some reason. This is especially helpful if you need to pivot quickly, such as was the case in Covid-19 times.

It's the businesses that stick rigidly to their original idea of what needs to happen which often lose their position in the market. Or indeed they never take off in the first place. The need to innovate, whether incremental or radical, needs to be constantly considered.

It was Stanford psychologist Carol Dweck who identified the 'growth mindset' as a factor in why some people don't give up on ideas or visions.[39] Dweck noticed that some students quickly overcame challenges and failures, while others wanted to quit after the first hurdle. She coined the term 'growth mindset' for those who have an underlying belief that effort makes them stronger and so are able to put in more time and effort in order to achieve their goals. In contrast, the 'fixed mindset' is possessed by people who believe they are born with a set of skills and who struggle to learn from mistakes.

There is no conclusion as to whether we are born with a growth or fixed mindset, but we can certainly nurture a growth mindset. In her research, Dweck referred to the brain's plasticity and our ability to consciously challenge ourselves. We can help ourselves to change our approach by rewarding ourselves when we succeed. Or at least we can acknowledge the success or do a deep dive into why something failed.

To nurture an open mind in business, here are key tips:

- **Be aware of your mindset.** If you are passionate about your idea, it can be a challenge to keep your mind open to changes for the product or service, because so much energy and effort has gone into

---

[39] See: Decades of scientific research that started a growth mindset revolution, *Mindset Works*, www.mindsetworks.com/science (accessed 19 March 2024).

creating the idea in the first place. Be aware of rigid thinking. Do you become defensive or annoyed if others question your ideas? Can you check in with people you trust to ask for a second opinion?

- **Celebrate the small wins.** If you have a new client or a new lead, or something happens that's not earth-shattering but still pleasing, take a moment to drink this in. Every success is worth acknowledging. Don't wait for the overall huge success before you stop to take a breath.
- **Assess as you go.** Keep on top of all the data. This includes research, feedback, customer reviews, etc. Without assessing what needs changing, you won't know what action to take.
- **Check in regularly with a trusted network.** Your support network is key when it comes to brainstorming, questioning and assessing so that you can keep making good decisions. Ideally, identify a mentor who is willing to be honest, and keep in regular touch.
- **Don't beat yourself up.** When things fail, which they will, choose to see this as a learning process. The scientific method and the entrepreneurial approach are both essentially the same – predictions followed by experiments to assess whether the theory underpinning the predictions is correct, followed by review and adjustments to the predictions if they prove wrong. **When something doesn't work, this is not failure.**

*

Over the years, I have funded start-ups with innovative ideas. My company ADI was set up based on the successful German model of Fraunhofer institutes, which focus on applied research, prioritizing key new technologies and commercializing their findings in business and industry. They are funded by a combination of private and public money and play a major role in the innovation process, with half an eye on their *Mittlestand*, small and medium-sized companies (SMEs). German SMEs are renowned internationally as having the strongest drivers for innovation and technology. It is these new developments that keep companies competitive and account for an extraordinary half of the country's economic output and almost 60% of jobs overall – an incredible achievement and one we could learn from in the UK.

This was the inspiration for ADI's approach of encouraging small business to creatively innovate. We wanted to find graduates or university students who want to pursue a big idea. This country is teeming with talented people, but investment is always hard to find.

Case study: tales from a mountain top

John Eaglesham is former CEO of ADI and now runs Breakthrough Leadership based in Shipley, West Yorkshire, helping more start-ups find their way. Here, he describes what he learned from his time at ADI, which ran for 15 years and helped numerous technologies to the market...

The first issue is to know your 'market fit' as the jargon says. What problem are you solving? Sometimes it's obvious but other times people get caught up, especially those working in tech, and get over-excited by the intrinsic elegance of an idea rather than the commercial merits.

You must be very clear who your customer is and have clear evidence people are prepared to buy your product or service.

Sometimes we cannot know until we try an idea. A clear example of this is when a clinician in Airedale hospital came up with an incredible idea to make remote consultations for patients easier. This was pre Covid-19, before it became more common and was quite groundbreaking. We pursued this, helping put together the tech so a patient could hook up with their doctor via their own TV set at home.

A lot of money and time was spent developing and integrating the technology, but very quickly two key problems were identified. The early concept was too challenging for patients to interact with easily, especially when they were unwell and on their own – if, for example, someone was recovering from a stroke and was required to follow instructions to connect some special hardware to the TV system for each appointment. It was too much of a strain. The second clear issue was money. Although it saved trips by ambulances to hospital in some cases, it simply wasn't financially viable.

However, instead of giving up, the innovators showed resilience and perseverance and pivoted. They spoke to potential customers and found a market in care homes instead. Next, they installed the tech into a series of care homes all over the country to experiment this way – and it worked. This was because care homes had on-site IT people or professional carers with experience to help make it work. The success meant the care home resident could get seen by a specialist by a flick of a button. Now more users had the tech installed, it made the proposition cost-effective.

One of the hardest parts of innovation is knowing when to hang on in there and when to give up. This is a deeply personal issue. I think most people hang on too long to a rigid or specific idea. The received wisdom is to 'fail but fail fast', but I would say 'learn and learn fast and change' rather than wait to fail. Put things to test cheaply and quickly, listening intently to what people say about your product.

Many make the mistake of being fixated on a particular way of looking at things. Their idea of persistence is bearing the pain until others see their vision. But in my experience, there is a tiny minority in this world who get it right first time despite everything; most of us mortals need early feedback and to innovate.

Confirmation bias

Further to John's advice, entrepreneurs need to watch out for confirmation bias in relation to their shiny new idea. Human beings tend to filter the world, looking for confirmation that things are how they see them. This could be via the echo chamber of social media (only following those who align with your own values or opinions) or only listening to comments or advice from people around you who want to please you.

We need to be able to widen our minds and our networks to really dig into ideas to know if they will work.

If you think there is a possibility the business plan won't work, then list all the cons and drill down into them all. What is the best-case scenario but also what is the worst-case scenario?

Flip the model too – look from different perspectives. Does it need more funding? Does it need a bigger market? Is it too niche? Introducing a brand-new product to the market means consumers will need education – are you in a position to do this with marketing?

John tells me that every entrepreneur faces these questions before their idea succeeds:

- When do you stick to your guns?
- When do you listen to feedback and adapt but hang on in there?
- When do you know it's time to stop and try something different?

Again, this is where the mentors and support networks can provide golden advice, especially if they possess practical knowledge.

The lean start up: another form of innovation

Returning to the idea of the scientist experimenting with a hypothesis, the business model for ADI was based on lean start-up principles (these are covered in a book published later, in 2011: *The Lean Start Up* written by Eric Ries).[40]

Reis talks about importance of 'validated learning', meaning using the scientific approach of making a hypothesis, then going out to test this on real people.

This is what we did at ADI with the telecommunications technology, as described in John Eaglesham's case study.

Reis talks about the need to provide the 'value' hypothesis to customers who are early adopters and the 'growth' hypothesis for customers in the wider market. He calls this the 'leap of faith', and both assumptions must be proven as quickly as possible.

Especially with market-led products, early adopters exist because the products are tested on key people who already share a similar passion. For example, if you started a company making fluffy dice and aimed it at a classic car event, you might shift a fair few straight away. But does the mass market

---

[40] See *The Lean Startup* website at: https://theleanstartup.com

want a fluffy dice revival? You need to know this information before you invest more money in making more of them!

If you can prove from the data that you have found early adopters AND a mass market, then investors will fly in. This is what happened to the inventors of Facebook. They encouraged their college friends to sign up and quickly entire colleges did so, and very early on they realized the proven market was potentially huge.

This ties into the idea of working 'smarter' and not 'harder' by working out what problem needs to be solved and then offering a minimal viable product (MVP) as soon as possible to the customer base. The MVP is essentially an early version of the product or service, something a customer can test and try and give feedback on in the very early days. The business can then pivot more easily, and unnecessary and expensive work can be avoided.

Reis calls this the 'Build-Measure-Learn loop'. You build the product, quickly show it to customers and get real feedback (not just online clicks, but information gained from talking to people) and then learn from what they say to change what needs to be changed.

He suggests making two different types of the product, with and without certain features, to see what is valued and what is not. This won't be necessary in many industries, but in some cases it can quickly identify what works.

The next step in the lean start-up is the 'pivot process'. He pans the age-old idea that a business simply needs a good idea and then nothing but perseverance is needed. Instead, Reis encourages the idea of 'pivot' meetings to discuss how to do things differently and better. This is exactly what we do at Surpass in our innovation committee.

Encourage innovation whatever stage you're at

At Surpass, we actively encourage innovation all the time, and everyone is welcome to pitch in. Innovation ideas should feel free and creative, because our thinking is affected if we fear being judged or ridiculed.

We have made 'ideas meetings' part of our mainstream business to normalize innovation. It's part of our open, honest way of communication. We can thrash out ideas and see where they land. At any time, we have around 10 innovations on the go.

On the committee, people suggest as many ideas as they like, even crazy ones. Many will be thrown out, but incredibly many of our madcap ideas have been developed. Incidentally, these only seem madcap initially – not after they get developed!

Over the years, our ideas have included:

- **Hearing test booths.** Using the same principle as a photo booth, a user can test their hearing without anyone else being present. We built a prototype, and the giant retailer Boots became interested, but the idea never took off. Twenty years later, hearing booths exist in places like Specsavers and Boots, so clearly our tech was too early for the market. This is a problem for many tech products, as it's very tricky to move from the early adopters (who are often tech-loving geeks!) to the mass market, where consumers might need educating about a product.

- **Training tablet.** We developed a prototype of what was essentially an early form of the iPad. It was a flat-top touch screen device designed for people to train efficiently in a certain industry. We got as far as showing off the model to Lord Sainsbury; however, we failed to raise the necessary investment. Then a certain company called Apple pipped us to the post.

- **Online invigilation.** This seemed like the wackiest idea in the world. Doing an exam at home? What madness! But, of course, people couldn't cheat any more than they could in person with others and cameras watching them closely. This idea took off during the Covid-19 pandemic. We now run this as a successful part of our online assessments.

- **Bird flu mitigations.** Years ago, I gave my elderly dad a role on the board to look at disaster and continuity planning, and he came up with the mad idea of mitigation against some kind of pandemic, like bird flu. He suggested developing emergency plans in case of a national lockdown. We all laughed but agreed that he could come up with a plan. One of his ideas was to create a strategy to allow employees to work from home, which we implemented. Years later, when Covid-19 hit, we were instantly able to put Dad's seamless plan into action, and I was the first to congratulate him on his foresight.

Covid-19 fast-tracked the ability to work from home for business of all sizes. Many have adopted the model long term, but also, the lockdowns from 2020 refocused many people's minds on what is important in life and what worthwhile wealth involves.

Spending time with loved ones and family, not having to commute and make unnecessary journeys, using local community facilities more and valuing spare time more has made many people reluctant to return to the office. Workers experienced a simpler life and saw how it could work better for their lifestyle.

Planting ideas

As noted already, the need for ongoing research is key at the beginning of any innovation stage. At Surpass, we refer to the desk research phase as the 'pot plant' exercise. This is the stage when we think of very basic ideas which act as our hypothesis.

Think of these ideas as seedlings. You plant loads of them, hoping one will germinate. Once you feel confident something is worth pursuing, it goes into the plant pot. Once it starts to grow, that's when it gets transferred to the cold frame, and this is where you begin to put significant investment behind it.

At the pot plant stage, we look at an idea and ask:

- How realistic is it?
- Do customers want it?
- What kind of investment is needed to implement it?

The pot plant stage is essentially to discover the MVP. This is the product that can be made quickly and with minimal cost, to be tried and tested as fast as possible.

The realism question is a central one. How realistic is your idea? For example, if there is already a clear market leader in the field, like the internet search engine Google, then forget it. Or if there is no competitor and your idea is a disruptor in the industry, would the market need education, or could you find investment to explore it further?

Some of the ideas I've had over the years were put back on the shelf. For example, I've got physics lessons on CD-ROM waiting (30 years later!) for the right moment in the market – which, with e-learning transformations and artificial intelligence, will come one day, probably quite soon. There is nothing wrong with keeping an idea on the shelf ready for when the market changes.

Timing

When starting a new business, you likely won't be juggling umpteen radical innovations at once. You're more likely to be focusing on the one big thing that will need adapting. It could be your product did well at the start but needs changing a year later or when the market changes unexpectedly.

In extreme cases, a market can change overnight.

For example, HF Holidays faced financial ruin when the foot and mouth disease outbreak in the early 2000s meant most countryside walks were banned. Quickly they pivoted and found alternative routes, such as pathways alongside canals, and offered holidays based on these instead.

At one point, BTL Publishing faced potential disaster too, when the most successful software companies abandoned the traditional development method, known as Waterfall, and adopted a method called Scrum. Essentially this is a process in which the specification of the software can evolve as the development proceeds, rather than being fully set out in advance. Around the world, companies were finding that the new approach led to better quality, faster delivery times and happier customers. However, this required a major retraining exercise for our staff, and we had to take an enormous gamble involving a six-month break to retrain everyone.

The need to innovate and quickly is why every business needs to keep track of changes and maintain flexibility to change.

History is littered with examples of established businesses that did not change or pivot fast enough. Nokia, for example, was the market leader in mobile phones, and their dominance seemed assured until Apple came along with truly innovative tech in the form of the smartphone. Nokia didn't adapt fast enough.

The late 19th-century proverb, said to have originated in Lancashire, 'clogs to clogs is only three generations' alludes to wealth earned in one generation seldom lasting through to the third generation. At the heart of this appears to be that the skill of innovation is lost from one generation to the next, and history shows success is hard to sustain unless you innovate and use energy and time wisely. This might be why the landed gentry keep hold of their brass and manage to hand their status down so easily. If land is kept in the family and not sold, it's easier to maintain and doesn't require much talent or thought to keep hold of it. That cannot be said of most forms of business.

Keeping your ear to the ground to find out what is happening in the market and innovating to keep ahead are key to maintaining your position.

Keeping on top of innovation

Key ideas to help promote innovation include:

- **Setting aside time purely for the innovation process.** Even if you are focusing on one big idea, keep looking at all elements. What is your competition doing? What is the market doing? What are the current trends? What do you envisage happening to the market in the future?
- **Considering new ways of making sales run more smoothly.** This can relate to using technologies. Would selling online make more sense? Would a new social media account reach the audience more effectively? Would outsourcing in a certain area help – for example, if your customers are all on TikTok but you hate filming yourself, could you afford help with social media?
- **Constantly keeping an eye on the market.** Try to avoid wasting energy on emotion around this (i.e. don't feel envious or annoyed you've missed a foothold), but look at it positively with an objective view. By researching, you can evaluate what you need to do better.
- **Being objective about potential innovation.** Seek out people who might not understand the innovation and practise explaining it. Listen to their opinions. You will learn to recognize the nay-sayers who are

cynical for the sake of it! Be wary of confirmation bias.

- **Considering innovation in business processes.** Innovation is not just about technology and new product ideas. In practice, a lot of innovative ideas relate to changes in business processes. Artificial intelligence is likely to lead to major changes in many areas. To take just one example, artificial intelligence can generate good-quality text from a few bullet points, and this is already changing the way many businesses generate marketing materials.

Further reading

Eric Beinhocker, *The Origin of Wealth: Evolution, Complexity, and the Radical Remaking of Economics* (2006).

Kim Chandler McDonald, *Innovation: How Innovators Think, Act and Change Our World* (2013).

12

Purposeful growth

In this chapter, I examine:

- Marketing a business to grow it
- Growing a purposeful network
- Growth as a leader

Walking for hours and miles becomes as automatic, as unremarkable, as breathing. At the end of the day you don't think, 'Hey, I did sixteen miles today,' any more than you think, 'Hey, I took eight-thousand breaths today.' It's just what you do.

—Bill Bryson[41]

When does a business need to grow? When you've got the hang of the day-to-day running? When the market or customers are demanding more? Or when it feels 'right'?

Before deciding, understand that growing your business is more likely to succeed if the growth is *purposeful* – that is, if it provides value, retains the 'why', and is good for other people, worthwhile and good for the planet.

---

[41] Bill Bryson, *A Walk in the Woods* (1998).

Growth for growth's sake is never a good idea. 'The pursuit of growth for its own sake is quite dangerous,' said Sir Roger Carr, Chair of BAE Systems,[42] and I agree.

Without a doubt, the model of growth that says it must come at all costs for a business, or a country, to flourish is now rightly being questioned.

As economist Manfred Max-Neef points out, nothing in the natural world, including our own bodies, grows endlessly. He adds: 'But we continue developing ourselves... So development has no limits.'[43]

The crux of this leads us back to flourishing. Let us learn to develop our business and our interests to flourish rather than for the sake of earning more and more money.

But how does an entrepreneur make the judgement call?

Overtrading is when the business grows too fast and cannot keep up with demand. But conversely if a business grows too slowly or remains flat, it will fail, because business is about adapting and being flexible to change, and no growth means no change.

There is a sweet spot to be found when it comes to growth *with a purpose*, but when is it time? Key signs include:

[42] MaryLee Sachs, Defining purposeful growth, *Forbes* (26 February 2016), www.forbes.com/sites/maryleesachs/2016/02/26/defining-purposeful-growth/?sh=45e11541fb4c (accessed 13 March 2024).
[43] Chilean economist Manfred Max-Neef: US is becoming an 'underdeveloping nation' [transcript], *Democracy Now* (22 September 2010), www.democracynow.org/2010/9/22/chilean_economist_manfred_max_neef_us (accessed 13 March 2024).

- When the pursuit of growth is not solely financially driven
- When the growth aligns with the vision of the founder or motivation drivers for why you set up the business in the first place
- When it's ethical and socially desirable – that is, when it doesn't pivot to harm others, or cause other harms such as increased waste or an environmental cost

*

At the point of making decisions on purposeful growth, an entrepreneur must know the business inside out to make informed choices. How is the cash flow? How is the market? Being on top of the data is key. If you're still not sure, then is the time to get outside advice – ask someone who has already set up a similarly successful business or seek professional advice.

Don't be afraid to change the original vision either. Whatever any company claims, most visions are tweaked and adapted to make the business work. This is fine if you can align them to your values and motivation drivers.

Some businesses simply don't need to grow in a traditional sense. For example, a mobile hairdresser probably won't gain anything from taking on trainees, because once they're trained, they're likely to leave and set up as a sole trader themselves.

Others, like the accountant Jane Ascroft, simply are not interested in growing any further than taking on a handful of staff. Jane's motivation driver was to keep worthwhile wealth at the forefront when it comes to business decisions, because she wants to pursue her other passions.

Making a judgement call about growth is one of the hardest, but most important, skills to have as an entrepreneur. The worst thing they can do is hide from the need to make the big decisions because growth of some kind is necessary.

Once again, consider the language used around decision-making. People fear failure deeply. When growth doesn't happen, we talk about having 'gone down the wrong path' or 'taken the wrong direction'.

Instead, adopt the scientist's approach again. When it comes to experiments, there are millions of different pathways to go down. To test a theory, we experiment, and if it doesn't work, we try another path. There is no failure here – only learning.

As C.S. Lewis said: 'We all want progress... If you are on the wrong road, progress means doing an about-turn and walking back to the right road; and in that case, the man who turns back soonest is the most progressive man.'[44]

Experimenting with growth might involve turning back and starting again in some way. This is where innovation comes into play again.

Key points when your business is ready to purposefully grow include when:

- You are unable to find time to prioritize the key decisions in the business. If you are juggling too many jobs, it's time to take on extra help. For example, the necessary task of bookkeeping is very time-intensive, but can be outsourced.

---

[44] C.S. Lewis, *Mere Christianity* (1960).

- You cannot keep up with sales demands. Examine cash flow and decide if you can afford to take on more staff or if you need a new supplier. Ask yourself if you're prepared to manage staff. If you are not, keep it small.
- You are re-examining the original reasons for starting the business. If growing bigger will impact your personal life negatively, consider pivoting in other areas and do not make it more labour-intensive.
- Customers indicate, through consistent high demand and repeat business, that they want you to grow.
- You have spare time. Growing will create new challenges – do you have the time to face them?
- You have to turn down business opportunities due to lack of staff or time.
- The market you're in is proving resilient and reliable infrastructure is in place to cope with demands.

If you are going to grow your business, it is important to ensure that all colleagues understand that growth is part of the 'day job' and not treated as something of an afterthought when all the day-to-day operational tasks have been completed.

At the level of a single business, it sometimes makes sense to grow rapidly, and sometimes it does not. Ultimately, it depends on what best allows you to achieve worthwhile wealth, including personal satisfaction, benefit to your community, sustainability and other factors discussed in the book.

This provides an insight into the idea of growth at national level. Such growth is not worthwhile if all it does is increase financial wealth and fail to produce worthwhile wealth.

Case study: tales from a mountain top

Ben McKenna is Chief Executive of Solidaritech, a company based in Bradford that refurbishes computers and tech for refugees. Ben grew this company after working within the tech industry for many years and spotting a niche gap in the market. He continues to work for his other company, a digital agency called Totaal, alongside growing this passion project. He has built a team of staff and volunteers, many of whom were refugees from around the world…

As a young lad, I grew up in a single-parent family, where my mum had to work several jobs to provide for me. I didn't like school and didn't do very well there, but luckily for me, Mum spotted the importance of other forms of education, including being computer-literate. She managed to save up from her three jobs and buy me a computer.

After leaving school with few qualifications, I still managed to find a job in the city thanks to my computer skills. Eventually, I worked for government agencies in the north of the UK and then became a web developer. Around this time, I became aware of how digitally excluded certain sections of society are, including refugees, and saw at the same time how companies were getting rid of their old tech in recycling dumps or in landfill. This revelation coincided with Brexit and I noticed the spike in hate crime, especially against marginalized groups. I wanted to make a difference, so began to try and persuade companies to donate their old tech, promising to wipe data and make them safe before passing them on to refugee charities. This grew organically into a new business, a passion project I called Solidaritech.

Finding donations was tough at the start, but word of mouth helped it grow. We have refugees from all over the world, many of whom are from different religions. For example we have Sunnis and Shias from the Middle East, who might not get on as neighbours in their home country but work together here. Regardless of which culture we're from, technology is always a leveller, because in this day and age it's what everyone needs. Many of our volunteers have received donations, which has helped them learn English, get a job or retrain, and they want to give back to the company.

I spend six months a year focusing on finding funding and six months building programmes, focusing on sustainable growth. What we do is to extend the life of the existing technology and not add to the five million tonnes of e-waste which currently ends up in landfill.

We have a clear purpose and are transparent about how many people we were helping and what donations were coming in on our website, solidaritech.com. Slowly it's grown and grown. We have refurbished and gifted over 1,100 machines this year (2023) alone.

I want to grow all the time, to help more people primarily. As long as we can offer a decent service at the heart of what we do, then growth is good.

For me, an absolute godless atheist, it's provided a deeper meaning to my life.

Marketing a business to grow it

Growing a business means telling more people about it. There is nothing as powerful as word of mouth, whatever the industry and however big or small the business. This is where values and reputation mean everything.

There are many free or cheap ways to advertise your business from the beginning – posting on social media, joining local networks, attending industry fairs, making connections and handing out business cards, having your story told in the local paper, even simply setting up a stand at the local school fête and selling your product there (if it's suitable!).

In my early days, I found out where GPs read about new technology and discovered they read two trade magazines, so I managed to get a piece written about my product in one of them. Every outlet helps!

However, the time will come when marketing needs to go to the next level. This advice dovetails with a lot of the advice around branding when starting a business. For example, you must have a website with good SEO rankings. This means that search engines are optimized to make it easier for online users to find you. Many consumers feel suspicious of businesses without any online presence at all. Growing a business could mean advertising the website, updating it or developing it further (hire a designer who specializes in this field, especially to help with key wording for SEO, etc.).

Other ideas include:

- **Creating a free Google Business Profile.** This allows you to create a new profile or manage profiles in Search and Maps.
- **Email marketing.** Can you send out regular updates or newsletters to existing customers?
- **Boosting paid adverts on social media.** This might include Google or Facebook ads.
- **Partnering with a relevant business.** For example, you may have some technology that would be of great benefit to someone with a sales-oriented business, and their sales channels may be of benefit to you, so you could work out a deal that helps both of your businesses. In practice, I have found that it is quite difficult to find a partnership that works equally for both parties, so scrutinize any possible deal carefully and ensure that both parties are willing to review whether it is working. Changes will be needed if one partner is driving around in a Rolls-Royce and the other has to make do with a wheelbarrow!

Also when you have experience of success, consider becoming a thought leader in the industry, sharing what you have learned in the market. This could involve sharing your ideas or thoughts via a blog or an online platform like TikTok or Substack, or through informative webinars. You could even offer to be a mentor to others starting out in the same field, to give back what you have learned yourself.

Growing a purposeful network

You cannot run a successful business without people, lots of people, at the heart of it. This could be customers, staff, other businesses, mentors or business networks. Does this sound obvious? It isn't to everyone. Many entrepreneurs I meet do not find networking comes naturally. They've often spent much time beavering away alone and struggle to communicate what they need to do to take their business to the next level. Whatever happens, finding other people to help you is what is necessary to move things along.

Being an entrepreneur can be a lonely business. Often the idea comes from you alone and unless you go into a partnership early on, all decision-making and donkey work will be yours alone too. That's why it's important to build a supportive, understanding, empathetic network from the off.

Successful places to meet like-minded people include: local business network groups – look for your local chamber of commerce or search sites like Eventbrite (www.eventbrite. co.uk) for established groups; Facebook groups covering your particular industry; and LinkedIn, which is a powerful professional platform. Make sure to regularly engage with others, post every week and comment on others' posts to create an impact.

The wider your network, the more likely it will succeed, because different people bring different skill sets. It's why diversity in business makes businesses stronger. Our business employs the most talented people we can find. We give jobs to people who are the best, and this automatically means we have a diverse workforce in terms of gender and ethnic background.

Once your business is established, consider if you have anything to offer your community. Could you offer to be a mentor to students in your field? Could you offer advice in some capacity to others?

The rewards of purposeful social connections

Social connections are known to be very good for our mental and even physical health. In Rose Anne Kenny's book *Age Proof*, she reveals how 80% of our ageing biology is due to lifestyle factors, including our social lives. In short, deep, fulfilling social interactions are one major factor to a long, healthy life.

Friendships and family relationships are definitely part of worthwhile wealth.

But also, social interaction can reap many other rewards. If someone likes you, or vice versa, they're far more likely to do business with you. Many of my business interactions have sprung from unlikely events and places.

Over the years, I have belonged to multiple networks reflecting my interests, from the Institute of Physics to The Alternative Board (an international business support network for leaders) to the Sheeptown Songsters to the Royal Society of Arts, Manufactures and Commerce (of which I am a Fellow). I've been amazed at how these diverse groups have helped in my businesses.

The following points describe some of the unexpected but purposeful connections I have made.

- In the mid-1980s, the UK government announced that it would set up a series of new schools called city technology colleges (CTCs), the forerunners of today's academies. The focus on technology aroused my interest, so I offered to be a consultant to these new schools. This resulted in me becoming involved in the CTC network, advising several schools and ultimately signing a contract to create on-screen aptitude tests for applicants to Dixons CTC in Bradford. This must have been one of the very first examples of on-screen assessment in schools.
- In 1995, BTL was situated in the Business Innovation Centre, near the University of Bradford and Bradford College. This led to a network of contacts at the university and the college, including in the college's economic development unit. As a result of these links, I was able to persuade the college to help raise funds from the European Union, matched by a contribution from local company Chase Advanced Technologies, to finance the founding of Virtual College.
- I joined a group of angel investors called NorthInvest, and they arranged for aspiring entrepreneurs seeking

funding to present to the group in the style of *Dragons' Den*. At one meeting, I was introduced to someone who thought that with my interests I should meet Phil Webb, who had a presence in the healthcare market. Phil subsequently introduced me to possible funders for ADI, and he himself became a director of the company.

It's not just business networks either. Once, after a long walk, I went into a pub in Coniston in the Lake District and spotted a chap sitting on his own. After grabbing a drink, I asked to sit by him.

Unbelievably, it turned out this fellow walker worked for a major internationally renowned brand and, not only that, was looking for a company to set up a multimedia service. A few months later, our company got the contract. Afterwards, I joked to staff that I should go on holiday more often! And to think I only went to talk to him because I felt like some company.

Tell the world about your venture, be proud of it and talk to anyone who shows interest – who knows what new pathways will emerge afterwards?

Clear communication

Be clear with what you want, especially if you're talking to other businesspeople or potential investors and mentors. If you do not communicate what you want and how you want it, then you're asking other people to guess what you're thinking. This is especially important in formal business settings.

It sounds obvious again, but British people can be very poor at communicating in basic language what we want for our businesses, especially when it comes to money matters. Asking for investment doesn't come naturally to many. Making a deal involves give and take and often compromise too. As the owner of the business, you need to be able to explain your pitch within seconds. Practising this pitch means you'll get it right, and the simpler it is, the better.

In every negotiation I take part in, especially with mergers or acquisitions, I encourage both parties to write down what their fears are, to kickstart an honest conversation. This is likely to reap rewards, because we can work out where the weaknesses are and address them.

Peter Brassey, my unofficial mentor, also taught me the need to 'get things out on the table'. If you have an issue or problem, don't understand something or want to challenge something, lay it all out there clearly and as early as possible.

Things can only progress if each party knows exactly what they're getting into and answers to questions are forthcoming.

Growth as a leader

The model of business is the Beatles. They were four very talented guys who kept each other's negative tendencies in check. They balanced each other and the total was greater than the sum of the parts.

—Steve Jobs[45]

---

[45] Steve Jobs offered rare insights during '60 Minutes' interview, *CBS News* (6 October 2011), www.cbsnews.com/sanfrancisco/news/steve-jobs-offered-rare-insights-during-60-minutes-interview (accessed 13 March 2024).

As soon as you consider bringing in staff, you're going to have to lead them. When staff work with the business founder in the direction of the grain of the business, delegation runs like clockwork. When staff decisions or behaviour go against the grain, suddenly the founder's time will be taken up with endlessly frustrating challenges. There are many books out there on management and this isn't one of them. Most tell you what to do and not what not to do.

My advice would be this:

- **Don't micromanage.** You have to trust your staff. I trust everyone until they give me a reason not to. It's impossible for a boss to be able to do the job of everyone on a team – that's why you employed them in the first place. Let them get on with the job. Trusting someone often inspires their trust.
- **Don't discourage innovation.** When you hire people to work for you, their ideas come free of charge. Indeed, most people are delighted when a company takes up their idea. The main issue is to ensure that innovative ideas are not filtered out before they get to you.
- **Don't be too risk-averse.** It's easy to be cautious about your business – too cautious, that is. That's because the sweet spot of growth relies on judgement. But mitigating risk is all you can do. Then you have to accept when a leap needs to be made.
- **Don't expect special treatment for yourself.** Whether this is in terms of parking space or special biscuits with your coffee, as the boss, it's the easiest thing to make demands. However, this will create a culture that doesn't make staff feel valued.

The power of humility

I had no training in how to be a boss or manager. Like leading walking groups in the hills, for me, it's involved learning on the job, making plenty of mistakes along the way no doubt. However, I always treat people as I would like to be treated and never expect any special treatment from staff.

When I became Head of Physics at Bradford Grammar, I took the worst lab in the department. If it was not good enough for me, then it would not have been good enough for everyone else.

Same with car parking, as first inspired by Peter Brassey. I don't have some specially designated space for my Jaguar to glide into every morning when I come to the office, aside from the fact I don't drive a Jaguar, but an old Volvo. I park in the same spots my staff use. Cath Bishop picks up on this point in *The Long Win*:

> At a superficial level culture is described in value statements placed on websites and desired behaviours assessed on appraisal forms. But it exists more powerfully at a deeper level inside human experiences of the workplace. It's the sort of thing you notice within an hour of visiting any business or organization. Who speaks first in the meeting? Do the more senior people in the office have reserved parking spaces near the door?... They tell us whether hierarchy dominates, which people are most valued and what behaviours are acceptable in practice.

If parking is a pain for the employees, the top dog needs to know about it.

I also like to encourage staff to take the credit for when we achieve success. Everyone's contribution is valuable, and they need to know they're valued. Listening to ideas, complaints, success stories and insights involves having an open-door policy regardless of what the issue is. This reaps rewards long term because you know what needs changing for the better.

Besides the respectful human aspect to this, it also means as a boss you know where improvements to the business need to be made. Being humble enough to hear others' viewpoints will only serve the business well and encourage growth that matters.

Further reading

Mark Mears, *The Purposeful Growth Revolution: 4 Ways to Grow from Leader to Legacy Builder* (2022).

Rose Anne Kenny, *Age Proof: The New Science of Living a Longer and Healthier Life* (2023).

13

The eco-entrepreneur

In this chapter, I examine:

- Why any new business must consider its environmental impact
- Whether net zero is achievable
- How eco-conscious businesses align with worthwhile wealth values
- Ideas for a green business

It would be meaningless in a book about finding worthwhile wealth with meaningful work to avoid talking about the biggest single threat facing us: climate change.

I do not consider myself to be an eco-entrepreneur per se, but in our businesses we constantly look at ways to improve our sustainability. I speak as a concerned citizen too, understanding we all have a part to play.

Sustainable means something different to ethical. Ethical focuses on human impact, whereas the common understanding of the term 'sustainable' in business focuses on not exhausting natural resources as well as on creating a successful business. Worthwhile wealth is intertwined with being eco-conscious. Inevitably, what is good for us is good for the planet. Psychologically, we feel better when we're having a positive impact on others and our surroundings.

Any long-term vision of a purposeful business must include consideration of the environment.

We are without doubt at a pivotal moment in our world's history. Weather patterns have changed dramatically, and we understand it's mainly human activity that's caused this. Staggeringly, the world's richest 10% are responsible for half of the planet's CO_2 emissions and it's the poorest nations that are hit the hardest.[46] This number will only increase, and rapidly. Some scientists believe the world is on course to becoming uninhabitable within even a century – we face a terrifying future with droughts, climate migration on a mass scale and water and food shortages.

But in the face of such challenges lies opportunities too. I often view entrepreneurs as little wind-up action figures who, given a problem, will set off to find a solution with energy and creativity.

Culture shifts slowly and then, often, suddenly all at once. I remain an optimist this will happen in increasingly momentous ways regarding the climate crisis. Think of the tobacco industry and cigarette smoking. It seems unbelievable today that we used to smoke on the Tube, on buses and in the cinema. Today it's viewed as socially unacceptable to

---

[46] World's richest 10% produce half of carbon emissions while poorest 3.5 billion account for just a tenth, Press release, *Oxfam International* (2 December 2015), www.oxfam.org/en/press-releases/worlds-richest-10-produce-half-carbon-emissions-while-poorest-35-billion-account (accessed 19 March 2024).

even smoke in your own home when visitors are present. A similar cultural change is happening in relation to fossil fuels.

Indeed, in 2023, UK academics urged the Royal Society, the association of the world's most eminent scientists, to condemn the fossil fuel industry, with 1,200 leading figures calling for an 'unambiguous statement' on climate change.[47]

Organizer of the letter, Professor Jason Scott-Warren, said: 'We need to see the gas industry in the same light as we now see the tobacco industry: sowing all kinds of misinformation and disinformation in order to keep on generating profits.'[48]

In the same year, the International Monetary Fund (IMF) found the total subsidies for oil, gas and coal in 2022 were £5.5 trillion – that's equivalent to 7% of GDP for the entire globe and almost double what the world spends on education. Ending the subsidies should be the centrepiece of climate action say the IMF.[49]

---

[47] Harriet Sherwood, UK academics urge Royal Society to condemn fossil fuel industry, *The Guardian* (23 August 2023), www.theguardian.com/environment/2023/aug/23/uk-academics-urge-royal-society-to-condemn-fossil-fuel-industry (accessed 19 March 2024).

[48] Quoted in Sherwood, UK academics urge Royal Society to condemn fossil fuel industry.

[49] Damian Carrington, Fossil fuels being subsidised at rate of $13m a minute, says IMF, *The Guardian* (24 August 2023), www.theguardian.com/environment/2023/aug/24/fossil-fuel-subsidies-imf-report-climate-crisis-oil-gas-coal?CMP=Share_iOSApp_Other (accessed 19 March 2024).

Also in 2023, 850 UK academics urged British universities to commit to plant-based foods only in their catering departments, to help reduce carbon produced by the meat industry, noting that these institutions have been 'the shining lights of intellectual, moral and scientific progress'.[50] As noted earlier, it's incremental innovations that keep the pace of change going.

With incredible change upon us, now is the time to consider seriously how our business will play a role in keeping up with the pace of this new low-carbon, climate-centred world.

Net zero

In a nutshell, net zero means slashing carbon emissions to as close to nothing as possible. Unbelievably, not all European countries have signed up to the net zero pledge, but in order to keep global warming to 1.5 degrees, emissions churned out need to be reduced by 45% by 2030 and must reach zero by 2050. While the energy sector is responsible for around three quarters of these emissions, they're also the industry that needs to drive the change to net zero, with renewables such as wind, solar and hydrogen.

---

[50] Damian Carrington, Hundreds of academics call for 100% plant-based meals at UK universities, *The Guardian* (4 September 2023), www.theguardian.com/environment/2023/sep/04/hundreds-academics-call-for-meat-free-meals-british-universities (accessed 19 March 2024).

Bob's musings from a mountain top

Can net zero be achieved?

As a physicist, I am often asked this question and the short answer is yes, but the long answer needs unpicking.

The most basic problem in achieving net zero is that of energy storage. Just as coal, oil and gas are fundamentally stores of energy (energy that arrived from the sun over many years in the past), we need to be able to capture and store energy from the sun as it arrives.

The key issues for net zero are therefore: whether enough energy arrives in real time from the sun to meet our needs; whether it can then be stored in such a way as to make it as useful and versatile as hydrocarbons, all without releasing CO_2 when the energy is released; and, finally, whether we have the knowledge to implement it. None of these issues need prevent progress.

The rate at which energy arrives at the Earth from the sun is vastly greater than the rate at which we convert this energy. This energy can be captured either directly by solar panels or indirectly through wind generators, and it is entirely renewable.

It can be stored in unlimited amounts by producing hydrogen through electrolysis. The energy can be recovered from hydrogen either by combustion or by producing electricity in a fuel cell (which therefore acts like a battery of unlimited capacity). Either way, there are no CO_2 emissions at all.

There has been lots of science and engineering work on these problems, and great progress has been made. In some countries, such as Denmark, Sweden and the Netherlands, electrolysis stations are being built. This is all good news, but problems we have in achieving net zero are largely infrastructural, and scaling up is a challenge for society.

In other words, saving the planet depends on leadership – that is indeed the hardest problem to crack – and will take time. Of course, we don't have much time or much good leadership.

Julia Davenport, in her excellent book *The Green Start-Up*, talks about this, having had personal experience setting up her former company Green Energy, which provides renewable energy. She calls the willingness to shift to renewables of the largest fossil fuel companies 'glacial'.

The main problem we face is that our national decision makers do not approach the problems in the same way as scientists, technologists or entrepreneurs. The process is adversarial, set up as a win/lose scenario with the best lobbyist winning the argument.

As Cath Bishop points out in *The Long Win*, this is no way to address the problems facing us. For example, the UK Energy Secretary announced in July 2023 that hydrogen will not be used to replace natural gas for home heating, amid concerns that it could cause major disruption.

However, he cannot possibly know this. The casual acceptance that growth in green hydrogen will be slow, when it is his job to ensure that it is not slow, is quite breathtaking.

Incidentally, most of the gas grid in the UK has been replaced with yellow polyethylene pipes that can readily cope with hydrogen, which was a major component of the town gas used widely until North Sea gas became available in the UK. The only sensible approach is to run the pilots with hydrogen boilers, along with the alternatives – heat pumps, direct electric heating and, of course, rapid insulation – as quickly as possible.

All environmental matters need urgent attention. The UK government's deferral of this decision until 2026 is both cowardly in the face of the electorate and grossly irresponsible in the face of obvious climate change. Unfortunately, it is also characteristic of a dysfunctional adversarial decision-making system. This kind of approach is hugely damaging to the prospects for net zero, and that is why 104 major companies wrote to the Prime Minister in July 2023 pointing out that the UK is being left behind on net zero.[51]

So, the short answer is that net zero can be achieved by the technology that's available, much of which entrepreneurs are working on. However, the long answer is we are still waiting for societal change, and leadership must be at the heart of this.

To be green or not to be green?

It's easy to still think: '*Well, what difference will my start-up make to climate change?*' The answer is: an awful lot.

However, the things individuals, small businesses, large businesses and society as a whole can do are all very different.

---

[51] Adam Vaughn, Net zero: UK is being left behind, big business warns Rishi Sunak, *The Times* (19 July 2023), www.thetimes. co.uk/article/net-zero-target-rishi-sunak-big-firms-companie-mbtkmjbgc (accessed 19 March 2024).

David MacKay, in his wonderful book *Sustainable Energy*, points out that 'if everyone does a little, we'll achieve only a little'. This is very important, and I used to think consequently that the efforts by individuals and small companies are of only limited value.

On the one hand, small energy savings here and there will not hack the problem; but on the other hand, individuals and small companies acting collectively can and should influence those able to have a real impact.

Of course, some small companies will grow into very large ones and have a direct impact. Look at Tesla, which came from nowhere and has completely changed the direction of the car industry.

The ripple effect of this will change decisions made at the top. I have seen this happen in my own companies.

We have incorporated what is known as a ESG (environmental, social and governance) into our strategy for years now. This involves a board that examines all areas of sustainability, looking at our emissions through our office and homeworking models, our carbon offsetting and our charitable contributions.

Over the years, our ESG approach has become increasingly important. When bidding for new businesses or completing supplier questionnaires from existing customers, we get asked what we're doing to be more sustainable. This is because increasingly it matters to customers and employees alike. The younger members of our workforce are at the forefront of driving change further and faster too. They demand better of the companies they work for, and we are reacting to this.

It's easy to simply pay lip service to sustainability or, in bigger businesses, to think it only really matters to the board that is dealing with it. But transparency around these issues will only be demanded more in the future. Examining what works and what doesn't is part of this.

For example, I felt uncomfortable about carbon offsetting flights when that idea came about, and wondered about their worthwhile impact. This instinct proved to be true, as many schemes are open to question now.[52]

Nobody has all the answers, but if we're adapting to create a business with minimal environmental impact, then we are contributing to a better world.

Consumer-driven change

A survey by Deloitte in 2021 found that around a third of UK consumers purposefully look for a brand with sustainable and ethical practices.[53] People are examining their consciences and lifestyle choices increasingly as awareness evolves.

---

[52] Patrick Greenfield, Revealed: more than 90% of rainforest carbon offsets by biggest certifier are worthless, analysis shows, *The Guardian* (18 January 2023), www.theguardian.com/environment/2023/jan/18/revealed-forest-carbon-offsets-biggest-provider-worthless-verra-aoe (accessed 19 March 2024).
[53] Shifting sands: how consumer behaviour is embracing sustainability, *Deloitte*, www2.deloitte.com/ch/en/pages/consumer-business/articles/shifting-sands-sustainable-consumer.html (accessed 19 March 2024).

As I have explored, small business is where change happens on a grassroots level, and that can have enormous impact. I have mentioned how SMEs are able to move fast and flexibly, having a direct impact on the local community. For example, small businesses tend to set up in buildings that are already available, and they use local resources and local networks. Small business can be more adaptable when it comes to working practices for those people who need flexibility. Experiments around better working practices are happening on bigger scale too, again involving small businesses.

In 2022, small companies, including a fish and chip shop in Norfolk and a software firm in Sheffield, were among 70 UK companies with over 3,000 workers that trialled a four-day week pilot scheme, set up by 4 Day Week Global in partnership with the think-tank Autonomy, the 4 Day Week Campaign and researchers at the University of Cambridge, the University of Oxford and Boston College.[54]

The trial was hugely successful. Staff surveys before and after the pilot found that 39% were less stressed, 40% were sleeping better and 54% found it easier to balance work and home responsibilities; also the number of sick days fell by

---

[54] Charlotte Lockhart, Results from world's largest 4 day week trial bring good news for the future of work, Press release, *4 Day Week Global*, www.4dayweek.com/news-posts/4-day-week-uk-results (accessed 19 March 2024).

two thirds.[55] A four-day week can no doubt create worthwhile wealth in some circumstances.

Most of the companies that took part reported they were satisfied with staff productivity and business performance. Many of them decided to make the change permanent. A four-day week isn't necessarily an environmental necessity (although reducing work days reduces travel and emissions from office buildings), but it proves change can be driven through quickly and have a valuable impact.[56]

Where to start?

There are so many schemes for environmental improvements in start-ups that it can be hard to decide what to do or know what is affordable. Julia Davenport's *The Green Start-Up* is a manual for companies, big and small, on what they can do to become as eco-conscious as possible, and this is a good place to start. I am taking note of what we can improve on too.

It's important to consider early on what your eco-conscious values will be, remembering there is always room for improvement. Among the many things start-ups can do are:

---

[55] Heather Stewart, Four-day week: 'major breakthrough' as most UK firms in trial extend changes, *The Guardian* (21 February 2023), www.theguardian.com/money/2023/feb/21/four-day-week-uk-trial-success-pattern (accessed 19 March 2024).

[56] Giada Ferraglioni and Sergio Columbo, The climate benefits of a four-day work week, *BBC* (21 February 2023), www.bbc.com/future/article/20230220-is-a-4-day-workweek-good-for-the-climate (accessed 19 March 2024).

- **Look at the overall carbon impact of the business.** Does your start-up cause immediate environmental damage? The National Federation of Self Employed and Small Businesses has good information on their website (www.fsb.org.uk), including a sustainability and net zero content hub.

- **Recycle.** Most of us do this anyway, but look at your product or service in detail, including any packaging or waste produced. Where can recyclable products be used? Can you go plastic-free? Can you compost at your business?

- **Measure energy use.** Can you use renewables? Save on water? Reduce emissions (for either delivery or production)? Can you work from home or consider how your product and processes can be tweaked to become more sustainable? For example, can you use e-marketing rather than direct marketing, reduce travel time or reduce energy wastage in the office?

- **Consider whether your product is long life.** Increasingly, consumers are turning away from the throwaway culture. How long is your product's shelf life? Can the product be disposed or recycled after use?

- **Examine your supply chain.** Really be honest about where you're sourcing your products. If, for example, you're setting up an ethical clothing company but importing cheap material from overseas, this will quickly unravel. Can you choose a local supply chain?

- **Use local products and facilities.** Where possible, can you use local sources or facilities, or employ local people? More networks of local green companies are banding together – how can they help you?

Early on, speaking to potential customers will always guide you. The cost of the product is important as well as its sustainability. There's no point producing a perfectly eco-conscious product that people are not willing to spend money on. Equally, it's not necessarily true that customers see cheap products as better. Often they have concerns that the quality is compromised, and the reputation of the product can quickly be questioned.

However, there could potentially be more help for start-ups that put green credentials at their heart. For example, the government offers tax relief and other benefits for companies that don't use much energy or buy energy-efficient equipment, and banks are offering 'green loans'. (You can find out more about grants and how other businesses can help here: www.greenmatch.co.uk.)

Case study: tales from a mountain top

It could be that, from the very beginning, your business model centres on green credentials or sustainable use. Sonya Bachra-Byrne and Liam Nathan Byrne launched a luxury womenswear brand with the idea of buying less, but buying higher-quality items, to counter the terrible waste of fast fashion. The company is called Avie (https://avie-studio.com) – the French word *avie* means 'for life' – and it's based in West Yorkshire. Their USP from the start was sustainability, and this meant they had to pay attention to detail. Sonya describes their approach...

I'd worked in New York and LA and the Far East for amazing fashion companies, but saw first hand the immense waste involved. So, when I decided to set up my own business, I wanted to counter this in every way possible. Even from a personal level, I do not like waste. I think it comes from having to clear my plate when I ate my dinner as a child!

We want to encourage consumers to 'buy better, buy less and buy seasonless', which means not being defined by trends. For every design, we ask ourselves when and where the customer could wear the garment, for how many occasions and why it can be something they can keep.

I had very little to no experience in sustainable fashion and really had to ask anyone who would listen for help and guidance. One person was Ian Rhodes, who I met through a business network. He provided the business outreach support for developing a network in the supply chain in the UK.

After setting up, we also got great support from AD:VENTURE in Leeds, who provide ambitious businesses with tailored support. Their expertise helped us to grow in the right direction and helped keep our business based in the local area.

At first, we used a factory in Romania as the UK factories did not cater for what we wanted with small production batches. However, with Brexit and Covid-19, we had to pivot quickly to the changes of the economic and retail landscape. At this point, reshoring production back to the UK and utilizing manufacturers in West Yorkshire and London became viable. Shipping and logistical costs had increased by 200% and using our European factories became untenable, and this led to what we initially set out to do: design and make clothing in Yorkshire to champion the textile legacy of this region.

We use high-end, eco-friendly materials like Lyocell, cupro (a silk alternative) and cotton. We also strictly limit the use of harmful chemicals and only use responsible UK and European factories that share our vision.

We even minimize the amount of fabric rolls we buy in and make sure we don't waste any of it, even making scrunchies or swatches from offcuts. Even down to the tags on the garment, we make sure they are recyclable paper, and we use pieces of rope.

Our label is something we can be proud of, because we are transparent with customers at every stage, utilizing some of the best European fabric mills that adhered to the 'Chemical management for sustainability' certification, which in 2019 was niche and an upcoming green credential.

In practical and monetary terms, it would be challenging for our small business to be 100% sustainable. But our mantra is: 'We do what we can, where we can.'

Plus the fact we have helped revive clothing manufacturing in a part of the country where it had died out is something that's very appealing to both industry insiders and consumers.

Putting the environment at the heart of your business

My brother Sam is another example of someone who changed the direction of his career due to climate concerns. After spending 20 years working for oil and gas companies, he got together with colleagues in 2007 to set up a carbon storage company, called CO2DeepStore. As he explained, he wanted to stop being part of the problem and be part of the solution. Sam's company was part of an early wave of groundbreaking companies that were trying to solve the problem of carbon storage and did very well, advocating the new carbon capture and storage technology to top government officials and big businesses.

The company was sold off in 2010 and Sam then helped set up Pale Blue Dot Energy, a leading provider of renewable planning and services. Today Sam is retired, but the company employs over 100 people and is still committed to tackling the ongoing challenge of climate change.

Ideas for a green business

There are huge opportunities for new entrepreneurs to develop start-ups in this sector. If you're still at the stage of considering what ideas to follow, the following ideas from Sam might spark something fresh and exciting for you.

- **Working in the circular economy.** Taking unwanted materials and reusing them or repurposing them is as yet barely touched, yet essential to our future.
  - One example, Revive (https://revive-eco.com), takes used coffee grounds and transforms them into useful products such as a palm oil substitute. Palm oil is currently used in very large quantities in the cosmetic and food industry, often with significant negative impact on the environment. A replacement is urgently needed. Used coffee grounds are often thrown away after use but can be reused in this way or as, for example, effective garden compost. This is a great example of a circular economy product with massive potential for reducing environmental damage.
  - Another example, Ferris (www.ferrisapp.co), has created an app for giving unwanted items a new home. It is a zero waste app for giving and getting for free. We all have things which we no longer use or need, and all too often they get sent to waste (recycling or landfill) when someone else might love to reuse them. Linking these two together is a major challenge, but critical if we are to address climate change and biodiversity loss.
- **Developing low-carbon energy.** This energy space is seeing a massive revolution as fossil fuels become unacceptable and low-carbon alternatives take over. The renewables space is well under development, but there are lots of opportunities in smart energy

(energy management, timing/phasing of energy use and energy storage, hydrogen, geothermal, heat pumps, etc.). There are also lots of opportunities for new business models.

Low Carbon Energy (www.lowcarbonenergy.co) offers low-carbon solutions for all businesses, from big companies like Boeing to small dairy farms.

- **Reducing energy demand.** This may look like an unlikely space for business, but there are a lot of emerging opportunities. Insulation to reduce energy demand in buildings is gaining traction with retrofit specialists, architects, designers and trades, as are devices which use less energy and energy recovery (e.g. heat pumps, solar and wind farms).
  - Buildpass (www.buildpass.co.uk) offers low-carbon retrofitting of older homes and say that a million homes will need to be retrofitted if we are to achieve net zero by 2050.
  - There are many niche companies popping up to help niche carbon issues. For instance, GreenStills (www.greenstills.co.uk) provides a technology solution to the Scotch whisky distilling sector, which enables significant reduction in process energy. This is done through a range of options, such as using heat pumps to recover waste heat, incorporating renewable energy in place of fossil fuels, energy storage and other process adjustments.
- **Impacting change through communication.** Examples in this field include education, consultancy,

coaching and delivering on climate action. There is a lot of opportunity to help leaders of other businesses, business teams, the public sector and individuals along the journey of change associated with climate change and biodiversity.

o For example, Force of Nature change (www. forceofnature.xyz) is a youth non-profit focused on education and coaching, transforming mindsets for climate action and helping young people move from climate anxiety to action. They also provide wider coaching and education programmes to help develop understanding and enable leadership on climate.

Avoiding greenwashing

Some companies are accused of greenwashing, which is when customers are deceived into believing a company's credentials have a bigger positive environmental impact than they actually do. Interestingly, the person who coined the term was the environmentalist Jay Westerveld, who spoke out about the 'save the towel' movement in hotels way back in the 1980s.[57] Westerveld argued the movement was not about saving water, but saving money for the hotels. Who knew!

---

[57] Lucy Siegle, Ethical living: is it worth reusing our hotel towels? *The Guardian* (23 September 2012), www.theguardian.com/ environment/2012/sep/23/lucy-siegle-ethical-living-hotel-towels (accessed 19 March 2024).

There are many examples of this kind of thing, although it is getting harder for companies to get away with it.[58,59]

A start-up involves a huge amount of planning, so it can be tempting to provide lip service to the green issue, especially when up against the costs of starting a new business. But thinking long term is once again key. Customers are increasingly looking for the sustainable options, so placing eco-credentials at the heart of any business is a wise decision.

Eco-entrepreneurism and worthwhile wealth go together

What makes us feel good in everyday life is often good for the natural world. By implementing ways to encourage worthwhile wealth in our new business, we boost productivity and morale and get to flourish in our working lives.

Eating fresh natural products, moving our bodies around using our own energy source, being outdoors, spending time with connected local communities, having work that's purposeful and brings satisfaction to other human beings – all of this is good for our planet too.

---

[58] ASA ruling on Innocent Ltd t/a Innocent, *ASA and CAP* (23 February 2022), www.asa.org.uk/rulings/innocent-ltd-g21-1111827-innocent-ltd.html (accessed 19 March 2024).

[59] Ed Davey, Shell's clean energy campaign is misleading, UK advertising watchdog says, *The Independent* (7 June 2023), www.independent.co.uk/news/shell-ap-london-advertising-standards-authority-youtube-b2353157.html (accessed 19 March 2024).

Take the example of transport. We run a 'cycle to work' scheme and provide discounted travel on local transport, both of which are arguably better for us. My wife insists we take the train when going abroad these days, and at first I was reluctant, thinking it would be slow and rather dull, etc. Her response was to ask why I need to run around everywhere like a scalded cat!

Tricia was right. Train travel is a joy. We end up chatting away to people, absorbing the local terrain out of the window and generally leaning into the slower pace of interesting travel. It's far more relaxing, far more connected, and preferable to the isolation and stress of going by plane.

Similar arguments can be made for a vast range of activities, including:

- **Reducing meat consumption.** The carbon footprint of meat is much larger than that of simpler foodstuffs, but in addition there is a known health benefit for reducing meat consumption.
- **Insulating your home to a very high standard.** This produces greater comfort and reduces CO_2 emissions.
- **Running a car powered by an electric motor.** This offers a much more pleasant driving experience and it is easier to learn in such a car. Pollutants from cars also cause damage to health, costing the NHS and society in general £6 billion per year.[60]

---

[60] Pollution from cars and vans costs £6billion per year in health damages, *University of Oxford* (6 June 2018), www.ox.ac.uk/news/2018-06-06-pollution-cars-and-vans-costs-£6billion-year-health-damages (accessed 25 March 2024).

We have implemented many schemes for our employees to show we value their efforts, and we also make the working environment as inclusive and enjoyable as possible. This in turn sparks loyalty and improved well-being for everyone.

Things like half days on Fridays, extra holidays according to length of service and the chance to 'buy' days off also matter to staff. We offer flexibility when it comes to bank holidays, which are traditionally catered around Christian holidays, so that religious festivals like Eid can be catered for. We provide free fruit in the office and free access to the Microsoft Enterprise Skills Initiative platform for training and development. These small perks add up to help our staff feel valued, which they very much are.

Anyone who goes into the mountains, simply by observing the way the glaciers have receded, has known for years that climate change is real. Ultimately, decisive environmental action will come not from governments, and only in a limited sense from individuals. The main driver will be businesses – existing large ones (like Tesla and Siemens) and fast-growing small ones which see needs and opportunities and aim to address them. One of my hopes is that this book will inspire you to play your part.

Further reading

Chris Goodall, *What We Need to Do Now for a Zero Carbon Future* (2020).

Marco Alvera, *The Hydrogen Revolution: A Blueprint for the Future of Clean Energy* (2021).

David MacKay, *Sustainable Energy – Without the Hot Air* (2016).

Mark Z. Jacobson, *No Miracles Needed: How Today's Technology Can Save Our Climate and Clean Our Air* (2022).

Ideas into action

At the summit of Ben Nevis, I got chatting to a fellow walker who took particular interest in my businesses. He wanted to know the steps I took and the secret to the success.

'But you don't seem like a usual businessman, if you don't mind me saying,' he said, laughing as we stood contemplating the view across a large part of the Scottish Highlands. I smiled and took this as a compliment. Then, he asked me a question I am often asked: 'How did you know back in 1978 that computer-based learning and assessments would eventually come along?'

The answer is I did not know for certain.

Indeed, many of the experiments I took proved to be dead ends (or unsuccessful experiments). However, it did seem inevitable that the power of computers would eventually throw up some major benefits in education, and I developed a passion to find out how. Work never felt like work, because through it I was following my natural curiosity.

I explained this to the man and told him that education, along with healthcare, is one of the most sluggish industries to adopt digitization that could transform learning outcomes. This is because education is run by the government, which has a top-down approach to innovation. Even though I have made it my life's work to help learning become more equitable, I've yet to see it happen in schools as I had hoped.

However, all the indications are that with the advent of artificial intelligence and full broadband multimedia, education will be dramatically improved through technology – my original vision.

That was my long answer. The short answer is that meanwhile I pursued other lines of innovation, which had real purpose to make people's lives easier, in businesses that fascinated me – all the while creating meaningful employment for staff who feel valued.

'I never expected things to work out the way they did,' I admitted, 'but I followed what I loved doing and ended up pursuing industries that interested me.'

Now in my early seventies, I am as excited as ever about the future, partly because work doesn't feel like work and partly because of the inspiring teams of people around me.

I am excited not only for Surpass Assessment but for the start-ups I invest in and for the future of entrepreneurism. We are at a stage when serious change needs to happen. It's my belief that us wind-up action men and women, us entrepreneurs, will be at the forefront of this supercharged change, creating not only a better world but a better way to operate our own lives too.

I hope any business ideas you have are spurred on to the next stage and beyond by the words in this book, both for the future of the planet and for you, the reader, whose life deserves to flourish and be filled with worthwhile wealth, in whatever form is most meaningful to you.

Questions to help decide on a business idea that creates worthwhile wealth – step by step

As well as the 'why' questions discussed in Chapter 6, you can use the following questions to help you think about business ideas for worthwhile wealth:

- What do you find in life that brings most joy and satisfaction? Is this something physical? Being outdoors? Helping others? Working with children or the elderly or animals?
- In an ideal world, where would you live? Write down the dream scenario – perhaps by the sea or in the countryside, or maybe closer to family or friends.
- What worthwhile wealth factors appeal most to you? More flexibility during the day? Being able to travel? Doing the hobby you love? Write down how you would ideally like to spend an average working day, from morning to evening.
- If you have extra time, what would you spend it on? Would you like to spend more time with family and friends? Pursuing ambitions? Travelling?
- What elements of your current job do you enjoy most? Helping people? Writing? Learning tech skills? The creative element?

- What skill set do you already have? Name the role you carry out and all the skills involved with this. Could you build on these with extra training or use your skill set to pivot to another role?
- How would your business fulfil the dreams you have set out? By allowing you to work from a laptop at hours that suit? By letting you work outside? By giving you freedom to work abroad?
- What is the simplest business idea you have? What problem does it solve for consumers?
- What business model is most appealing to you? Working solo, working with a partner, employing people?
- What comparable business is already in the market and turning a profit? Look it up and see if you can speak to the founder to ask them what their challenges were. Could you do anything differently or better? Or is there room in the market for a more local alternative?
- What do you fear most about trying to start this business? Be honest. Is it lack of experience? (Can you research how to gain experience?) Is it loss of status? Is it lack of funds/time/head space? Whatever the obstacles are, naming and recognizing them is halfway to finding a solution.

Setting up step by step

Step 1

1. Write down the exact vision of your dream business.
2. Return to the 'why' question to decide its purpose.

3. Find potential customers, where possible, to ask what their needs are and how your business will relieve the pain point.

Step 2

1. Start to consider a business plan. Do you need an official plan?
2. Identify funding options (investors, early investment from family and friends, self-funding, grants, bursaries).
3. Identify the most suitable business structure (limited company, sole trader, partnership).
4. Do a monthly cash flow forecast.
5. Hold 'board' meetings – even if it is only you there – and record decisions made.
6. Focus on what you must do to get sales on the planned timescales (which could take a long time if you have to develop your product).
7. Ultimately, remember that without sales there is no income, and without income there is no business.

Step 3

1. Rally support from family and friends, and local networks.
2. Find a trusted mentor.
3. Consider how to, or if you need to, build an MVP (or service) to test early on.

Step 4

1. Identify the main risks of this business idea.
2. Put together a basic mitigation plan.
3. Where appropriate, create an MVP (or service) to test on consumers early on.

Step 5

1. Work on branding – though it may have to wait if your 'why' is not clear.
2. Consider company name, and register at Companies House.
3. Use professionals, if need be, to develop a logo and brand vision, and to set up a website.

Step 6

1. Get going!
2. Make changes based on what you learn from customers' reactions to the MVP or the service you offer.
3. Keep asking your customers for feedback. Never stop.
4. Keep incremental innovations in mind.
5. Make the business work for you, not the other way around.
6. Keep going!

Remember: Nobody is saying it is easy, but by thinking about the things covered in this book, you can certainly make sure it is worthwhile.

Appendix: Bob's journey – step by step

How does a physics teacher become an accidental entrepreneur? In the following, Bob describes his early life, then provides CVs covering his 'unlikely entrepreneur' journey and his 'worthwhile wealth' journey.

Early life

August 1950 — I was born in Morley, near Leeds, to parents Joy and Tom Gomersall. Dad is the first person in his family to go to university, where he studied physics. He reluctantly joins the family-run soft drinks business, in which he has a minority stake. I decide at an early age that business isn't a life for me.

1959 to
1976

I attend Leeds Grammar School, then study Physics at Durham University and complete a PhD in Theoretical Physics at the University of Bristol before becoming an academic, holding a Royal Society European Fellowship at the Max Planck Institute, Stuttgart.

Academic life gives me the confidence to question received wisdom and allow myself to show enthusiasm. Students from all over the world teach me that it's a peculiarity of British people to be suspicious of excitement! I also learn that research can indeed be phenomenally exciting. It's a great feeling to know that you have discovered something no one else in the world yet knows.

A path towards becoming a professor is the natural progression, but my personal life intervenes. My wife, Tricia, begins her training as a GP, and in search of a more settled life, we return to the north of England to live. This is my favourite part of the country, with its access to walking in the Dales and in the Lake District.

1977 to
1997

I leave academia behind and retrain as a teacher, becoming a physics teacher at Manchester Grammar School. A few years later, I get promoted to Head of Physics at Bradford Grammar School and spend the next 17 years there. A job for life? It seemed so.

I love teaching and spending time with teenagers, who never fail to make me laugh. However, teaching methods in schools seem stuck in the past and I begin to wonder how teaching can be improved and how learning can become more accessible for everyone.

The unlikely entrepreneur CV

1978   Working with some of the first desktop computers, I begin to tinker with ideas. I believe one day everyone will have access to a home computer. Inventing online lessons is a big idea, and it starts brewing. So, I experiment in my spare time.

I create a series of A level tests to run on the Manchester Grammar School minicomputer. I then convert them to run on one of the first desktop computers, the Commodore PET.

Boom! Hugely proud of my new product, I can't wait to approach the relevant markets: examination awarding bodies and publishers. But when I share my idea with a northern examination body, they reject it outright.

I consider setting up my own publishing company; however, pursuing two big business ideas at the same time feels likely to end badly. So, I park computer-based testing to focus on electronic equipment. This idea is gaining traction... in any case I need to learn more about electronics.

1984

My early inventions include a veterinary respiratory monitor and a car warning light, but alas I can't find a market for them. I need something that's easy to make and will sell in small numbers but provide a large margin.

That summer, I go for a walk and end up chatting to an old friend, Dr John Thompson, a GP in North Wales. Bemoaning my lack of success, he makes a suggestion: 'Why don't you try making audiometers, used to test hearing, that are easy enough for GPs to use? We're short of those.'

Little did we know this conversation would change the course of my whole life.

I go home and start work. Eventually, I get my hands on an audiometer and open it up. I reckon I have the skills to make this machine simpler to use and simpler to build. Suddenly, I've found a potential product with a proven market.

1985

I show a prototype to a council funding scheme and receive a grant of £400 to make two more – the most productive sum of money ever! I set up Bradford Technology Limited (later BTL) as a company to pay in the grant. After school and at weekends, I roll up my sleeves and start making the audiometers piecemeal, with help from Mum and Dad.

Over the next few years, the business steadily grows. I watch the online learning space develop too, after the invention of the CD-ROM.

By the late 1980s, CD-ROMs have gained global popularity, which gives me ideas for new products.

I begin to experiment with online lessons again, creating early forms of multimedia to make them more fun and accessible, and I look for ways to publish these.

1989 ● BTL wins its first major contract, to develop a series of aptitude tests in a brand-new local school, Dixons City Technology College (now Dixons City Academy). I recruit students to generate the content, including a former pupil of mine, John Winkley, who is smart and enthusiastic about the products.

Our next product nearly breaks the company. We set up a simple language learning programme alongside a paper manual. But I have no idea how to get a book printed and fail to proofread it properly so have to pay for another expensive print run.

1992 ● By now, I need full-time staff. I employ two people to deal with administration and technology. I warn them I have no idea where this business is going to go, but I still have big ideas and a passion for education.

As the audiometers sell, we also develop an on-screen teaching tool that involves text, audio, animations, video, simulations and quizzes. Then laser disks come onto the market, meaning more storage for such a product. However, deciding which kind of CD laser to place our product on is excruciatingly difficult, because I have no idea where this new technology will go.

Luckily, I choose the right one. We decide to put my lessons onto CD-ROM.

I raise cash from family and friends in return for a small number of non-voting shares in the company.

I rope in my brother Bill to design the graphics. The first title, *Electricity and Magnetism*, 1992, is one of the world's first multimedia learning titles on CD-ROM. I sell these products directly to teachers at educational shows and through direct mail.

1995 — I set up Virtual College Ltd (later Virtual College PLC) to run a vocational training project, for which I win funding in partnership with Bradford College and another company, Chase Advanced Technology. John Winkley agrees to run the project, and then Rod Knox joins and takes on the role of CEO.

My dream that education can be made more accessible to everyone is coming true.

1997 — I take a leap and begin publishing under the trade name of BTL Publishing.

Our CD-ROMS sell well, and I embark on new titles, including the Complete Physics series.

Determined to give this new business everything, I leave teaching to focus on it full time.

We win fantastic contracts for rights to the *AA* and *Mr Men* books, to produce their products on CD-ROM. Peak sales grow to £2 million.

1999 This is a pivotal year. The BBC suddenly announces a plan to enter the education technology market for schools, and boom! The entire market collapses as sales dry up for the smaller companies. Pearson, a rival, takes them to court, and eventually the BBC backs down, but the damage has been done as most schools stop buying products until it's clear which way the wind is blowing.

BTL Publishing continues in a more limited form, and Virtual College, offering vocational training using e-learning, continues to grow. Meanwhile BTL, guided by CEO Keith Myers, makes the decision to swiftly pivot to online assessment. This proves to me how important it is to be able to innovate in a business!

Over the next decade, Virtual College develops a range of ready-to-go multimedia titles that train people for jobs in a wide range of areas, including healthcare, safeguarding children and adults, and food and drink. We build up a customer base of 3.5 million customers.

These innovations, especially in the approach to the market, are crucial, and BTL rapidly grows as a leader in online assessment, which remains the core part of our business activities to date.

2005

I set up ADI (Advanced Digital Institute and, later, Advanced Digital Innovation) to encourage innovation, especially from graduates and people with special interests. Anyone is welcome to pitch.

We specialize in advanced electronic design, and technology applied to healthcare and smart energy, and become a leader in telehealth, assisting communication between doctors and patients.

One of our breakthrough products is tech allowing doctors and patients to communicate via an app instead of relying on letters in the post. With this app, eventually called MyPathway, patients can track their appointments and their doctors' feedback, access resources and complete pre- and post-treatment questionnaires. The process helps the hospital run smoothly, because nothing gets lost in the post, and the data helps review patients' overall experience and inform the hospital on the effectiveness of treatments.

2017

BTL Group Ltd sets up a successful US subsidiary (Surpass Assessment Inc).

BTL becomes a provider of e-assessment technology to most major UK awarding bodies, and a number of major professional associations worldwide, including the National Board of Medical Examiners (US), CPA Canada (chartered accountants), the Caribbean Examinations Council, ICAEW South Africa, the American Bar Council, City & Guilds, the AQA, the SQA (Scottish Qualifications Authority), Cambridge Assessment, the WJEC (a Welsh awarding body), the TDA, the AAT, the British Council and Pearson. Meanwhile Virtual College continues to grow rapidly.

2021   Virtual College is acquired by Netex Learning, a listed Spanish company.

The same year, BTL wins the Queen's Award for Enterprise (International Trade).

I am named as the first winner of The e-Assessment Association's Lifetime Achievement Award.

BTL starts to use the trading name Surpass Assessment, the name we use today.

2022   MyPathway is acquired by a Canadian company, VitalHub, and a new company, MyPathway Solutions is set up, adopting the name of its main product. The revolutionary technology of MyPathway is currently used by patients in leading Sheffield hospitals.

2023   Surpass remains a world-leading computer solutions business, and our head office is still in West Yorkshire. Our latest product includes a groundbreaking artificial intelligence software called Surpass Copilot, which creates better test questions faster and at less cost.

We continue to innovate in areas of education technology, with my unwavering vision being to make personalized learning accessible to everyone.

Worthwhile wealth CV

1969
I join HF Holidays Ltd, a not-for-profit company that organizes walking holidays. I become a mountain leader aged 18, and although I have a lot of mountaineering experience it is still the steepest learning curve I've ever been on!

But my deep love of walking outdoors begins; I find companionship and a passion for life.

I meet Tricia, another member of staff, and we get married. So many walkers meet their partners here – it's known as 'Husbands Found'! Tricia and I have four children together.

1978
I am elected to the board of directors of HF at the age of 28.

1983
I am elected HF Chair.

Over the years, HF Holidays wins many awards, including Guardian/Observer Best Large Tour Operator, and it has been a Which? Recommended Provider since 2013.

It is a cooperative with 30,000 shareholding members and provides 55,000 holidays (mainly walking and activity) every year on a worldwide basis. I occupy the role of Chair for several terms, totalling 10 years.

My passion for walking in the great outdoors means twice a week I walk around the local area with the Bradford HF Walking and Social Club. We also go on walking holidays two to three times per year, visiting different countries – to date, Austria, France, Germany, Italy, Poland, Spain, Switzerland and Turkey.

1999 ● Yorkshire Forward, the regional development agency, appoints me Chair of their Digital Cluster, which encourages the development and growth of digital businesses in the region.

2000 ● I become a Fellow of the Royal Society of Arts, Manufactures and Commerce.

2001 ● I join Bradford Breakthrough, a group of local businesspeople who work together to make Bradford a great place to live and work.

2002 ● I am appointed Chair of the Scout Executive for the 1st Ben Rhydding Scout and Guide Group. I want to give something back, having been in the Scouts as a child. All my children were in the Scouts or Guides and got so much from the experience. My role coincides with Scouts and Guides merging into one group, so I help with this process and encourage them to improve their headquarters.

2011 ● I become an ex officio member of the newly established Leeds City Region Local Enterprise Partnership.

2015 ● I learn to sing and join a local natural voice choir. This is another very steep learning curve, but a surprisingly enjoyable one. I have since sung in many notable places, including the cellarium at Fountains Abbey and Skipton Town Hall and, most memorably, at my daughter's wedding, where Tricia and I sang 'A Gaelic Blessing'.

2016 ● I become Chair of Bradford Breakthrough.

2021 ● I am appointed Vice-President of HF Holidays.

2023   ●   The Entrepreneurs' Forum, a networking organization for all entrepreneurs to meet and support one another, is created.

Acknowledgements

This book could not have been written without the fantastic work of my ghostwriter Shannon Kyle, who has not only provided indispensable input but also provided motivation and inspiration when my own enthusiasm dared to flag. Her guidance has been invaluable.

I am also very grateful to Sally Abbatt, who works with me on all my business projects and helps look after my family's interests. She has managed the administrative side of things with her usual efficiency and has provided valuable advice at every stage in the process, especially when she thinks my opinions need to be corrected.

In addition, I am grateful to friends and acquaintances who have been willing to allow their personal 'case studies' to be included in this book, and to do so in a spirit of openness.

I have over the years had many advisors and I am especially grateful to our family advisor, David Dickson, and to my colleagues in The Alternative Board, with whom I have been able to share my successes and failures over many years and whose support has been fantastic. They include Paul Dickinson, Jo Clarkson, Ian Thompson, Gary Parlett, Martin Allison, James Cain and Jon Whiteley.

I will always be grateful to former Headmaster David Smith and the governors of Bradford Grammar School, who tolerated my business activities while I was still in post as Head of Physics. I hope they feel they have been repaid many times over by the impact on the Bradford economy of the many jobs created, and hopefully by the impact on education more generally.

Finally, I am grateful to the many talented executives I have depended on over the years. Early on, I decided I was not cut out to be a chief executive, and so their contribution has been critical. I am particularly grateful to those that have had a major influence on my own thinking, including Peter Brassey, Brian Smith, David Harrington, John Winkley, Rod Knox, Lesley Ord, Keith Myers, John Eaglesham, Sonya Whitworth, Andy McAnulla and Jim Crawford.

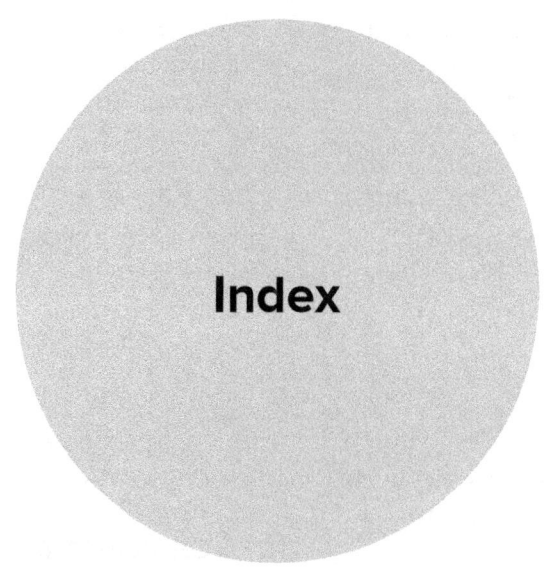

Index

A quick word from Practical Inspiration Publishing...

We hope you found this book both practical and inspiring – that's what we aim for with every book we publish.

We publish titles on topics ranging from leadership, entrepreneurship, HR and marketing to self-development and wellbeing.

Find details of all our books at: www.practicalinspiration.com

 Did you know...

We can offer discounts on bulk sales of all our titles – ideal if you want to use them for training purposes, corporate giveaways or simply because you feel these ideas deserve to be shared with your network.

We can even produce bespoke versions of our books, for example with your organization's logo and/or a tailored foreword.

To discuss further, contact us on info@practicalinspiration.com.

 **Got an idea for a business book?**

We may be able to help. Find out more about publishing in partnership with us at: bit.ly/PIpublishing.

Follow us on social media...

 @PIPTalking

@pip_talking

@practicalinspiration

@piptalking

Practical Inspiration Publishing